Weedless GARDENING

BY LEE REICH

Illustrations by Michael A. Hill

WORKMAN PUBLISHING • NEW YORK

Library of Congress Cataloging-in-Publication Data
Reich, Lee.
Weedless Gardening / by Lee Reich.
p. cm.
Includes bibliographical references (p.).
ISBN 0-7611-1696-6 (alk. paper)
1. Weedless gardening. I. Title.
SB453.R414 2001
635'.0481—DC21   00-043512

Workman Publishing Company, Inc.
708 Broadway
New York, NY 10003-9555
www.workman.com

Manufactured in the United States of America
First Printing January 2001
10 9 8 7 6 5 4 3 2 1

DEDICATION

To my wife, Deb, who likes
gardening, and to my
daughter, Genevieve,
who loves books.

TABLE OF CONTENTS

❧ CHAPTER SIX ❧

❧ CHAPTER SEVEN ❧

EPILOGUE

APPENDIXES

INTRODUCTION

How We Got Here

L et's blame it on Jethro Tull. He was the 18th-century farmer and writer who advocated thorough pulverization of the soil on the (wrong) assumption that plant roots could most efficiently gobble up the resulting small soil particles. That is one reason why, each spring or fall, gardeners go out into their gardens to turn their soil over and over, only to battle weeds throughout the season.

This conventional way of gardening *does* welcome in the growing season with a clean slate, but the benefits are transitory. Don't weeds always seem to return with a vengeance? In a new garden, growth of vegetables and flowers will be especially lush following a thorough "working" of the soil. But this benefit is also deceiving, the result of too much air pumped into the soil suddenly mobilizing great reserves of nutrients. The situation becomes akin to withdrawals outstripping deposits in a bank account.

Enter Weedless Gardening, only one benefit of which is fewer weeds and less time spent fighting them. The essence of this new way of gardening is to care for the soil from the top down. All feeding is done at the surface, which is always snuggled beneath a protective, perhaps

Basic Weedless Vocabulary

TILLAGE: turning over or otherwise churning the soil

CULTIVATION: 1. syn. TILLAGE; 2. for our purposes, the general care of plants

ORGANIC MATTER, ORGANIC MATERIAL: living and once-living materials in various states of decomposition

HUMUS: the relatively stable end product of decomposed organic matter

WEED: a plant in the wrong place

MULCH: any covering on the soil, whether living, dead, natural, or synthetic

nutritive, "cover." The particular cover might be a mulch of compost or wood chips or living plants—depending on what you're growing and how you want the garden to look. Annual disruption of the soil (whether by rototiller, plow, or shovel) is eliminated so the soil can develop and maintain the layering found in its natural state. The result: nutrients, air, and beneficial humus become most abundant at or near the surface, where plant roots naturally proliferate.

Weedless Gardening springs from very old methods, so old that they might well be considered new. Perhaps the best, and surely the oldest case to be made for gardening this way—from the top down—comes from Nature. Just look to the forest or the prairie or the meadow, where the soil is undisturbed and nourishment from old leaves, stems, and roots accumulate at the surface. How well plants grow there, with little regard to whether the season has been warm or cool, wet or dry. For the starkest contrast, take a look at the lush green weeds flaunted by Mother Nature in the uncultivated border of a parched garden or farm field during a dry summer. Aren't those weeds and the soil in which they grow saying something?

Primitive cultures lacking the rototillers, digging forks, spades, and other tools of modern gardeners and farmers have always had no other choice but to care for their soil from the top down. After all, how much dirt can you stir up or turn over with a pointed stick or an animal bone poked into the ground or tugged through a field?

The lay of the land is what prompted early farmers near present-day Mexico City to develop their version of gardening from the top down. There, a naturally broad expanse of shallow water surrounded by arid land was turned into a patchwork of islands and canals. This landscape was created and maintained by scooping mud and vegetation up from the waterways to form the islands of rich soil. Capillary water oozed up to plant roots from below, or water could be conveniently dipped from the canal with a bucket. Weeds were few because the soil was regularly topped up with new mud and vegetation. The remains of this agriculture can be seen today in the so-called floating gardens at Xochimilco.

Even in modern times, the occasional gardener or farmer has rallied against

Weeds thrive in the untilled soil bordering a tilled field of wilting corn.

excessive disruption of garden and farm soil. In his 1943 classic *Plowman's Folly,* Edward Faulkner answered his question "Why do farmers plow?" with nothing more than "Farmers like to plow." Is there some primal urge that prompts all of us to stir the soil in spring and then sit back and admire the clean expanse of soft brown earth? To both lessen weed problems and help plants survive on less rainfall, Faulkner suggested abandoning the plow for the disc. This tractor-pulled implement breaks up only the surface of the ground, cutting any existing vegetation into the top layer with gangs of weighted, rolling metal discs.

Beginning in the 1950s, weeds, water, and a desire to make gardening less work prompted Ruth Stout (chronicled in *How to Have a Green Thumb Without an Aching Back* and *The Ruth Stout No-Work Garden Book*) to tout a gardening system of doing nothing more than blanketing the ground with hay. (And plenty of it—about 25 bales annually for a plot 50 feet by 50 feet.) She poked large seeds right into this tawny blanket, but parted the hay and created little peat-moss beds for small seeds. Weeds that appeared were either yanked out and laid down to add to the covering, bent over and smothered with more hay, or discombobulated as the hay was purposely fluffed up by Ms. Stout's pitchfork. With no disruption of the natural layering of the soil and the permanent hay blanket, water needs and weed problems were minimal.

Across the Atlantic in Britain, Rosa Dalziel O'Brien described yet another variation on this theme in *Intensive Gardening* (1956). Rather than being allowed to intimidate, weeds were allowed to grow to a certain extent under a watchful eye to shelter crop plants, to balance soil fertility, and in an ironic twist, to provide material for compost to feed future plants when spread on top of the soil.

The cry for minimizing soil disturbance and for protecting the soil's surface continued to be voiced. Plant health, soil health, and less work are the attractions. Masanobu Fukoka, in *One Straw Revolution* (1978), took a laissez-faire approach to his rice farm by tossing out seed for the next crop in among standing stalks of the harvested crop.

Robert Kourik (*Designing and Maintaining Your Edible Landscape Naturally,* 1986), Patricia Lanza (*Lasagna Gardening,* 1998), and others have advocated starting a garden with a layered sandwich that includes fertilizers, grass clippings, leaves, manure, newspaper or cardboard, compost, wood ashes, and sand.

To round out the possibilities, I am reminded of a friend's ultimate variation on the top-down theme, practiced decades ago: He simply used a lawnmower to cut back weeds that grew up between rows of vegetables. University research on the possibilities of "living mulches" for farms and orchards no longer make this idea seem so far-fetched.

What is now needed, rather than to blame Jethro Tull or take random stabs at maintaining the integrity of the soil, is a workable alternative to the conventional way of caring for our soil. Going back to pushing or pulling a pointed stick or animal bone through the soil is not the answer; these are inefficient tools that try to

Laying straw on the ground can kill weeds, just like a rototiller or spade, but works most effectively when integrated with other Weedless Gardening practices.

do what rototillers do better. Few of us garden in shallow water, where we could emulate the canals and islands of Toltec and Aztec gardeners of hundreds of years ago. And as for Edward Faulkner's disc? It had potential on a great spread of farmland in the 1940s, but it's not a tool that you're likely to find in the garden shed of today's backyard gardener. Ruth Stout's methods work fine if you have a sandy soil that won't pack down as you tromp all over it year after year, and if there are no stumbling blocks to getting bales and bales of hay into your garden each year, or if you have, as Ruth did, a hayfield and someone to cut it right next door. Fukoka's methods are hardly adaptable to growing anything beyond citrus and grains. And layer upon layer of organic materials might be a way to start a plot of vegetables, but such a system needs to be elaborated on to be useful year after year and with other plants.

In the pages that follow, I have drawn from what has been tried by gardeners and farmers—and from what I've observed and learned from Nature—to synthesize something new, a system of growing I call Weedless Gardening. Integrated parts of this system meld together to create gardens that are good for the plants and good for the gardeners. With some wrinkles, it can be applied just about everywhere. My tools have not been pencil, paper, and computer, but rather trowel, pitch-fork, and garden cart. More than two decades of experimenting and fine-tuning this method of gardening from the top down have shown benefits not only to plant and soil health, but a dramatic enough reduction in weeds and weed problems so that the system can truly be called Weedless Gardening.

CHAPTER ONE

·····································

Why Garden from the Top Down?

An unintended effect of turning over or stirring up the soil is, essentially, to sow weeds. Rototilling, plowing, and hand-digging will bury and uproot existing weeds, but these activities also expose to light and air the many weed seeds (140 per pound of soil by one count) lying at various depths within virtually every bit of ground. Sun and oxygen are just what these weed seeds have been waiting for to sprout.

Not all weeds start out as seeds awakened from within the soil. Weeds also sprout from seeds that are carried into the garden by wind or hitchhike on (or within) animals. A thin mulch over the soil, renewed yearly, takes care of most weeds that arrive in this manner.

You cannot, of course, just banish the words *rototill, dig,* and *plow* from your vocabulary, throw some mulch on the ground, and carry on with your gardening as before. These practices, for maximum benefit, need to be integrated into a Weedless Gardening system. The bare bones of Weedless Gardening, elaborated on in coming chapters, have four components.

1. MINIMIZE SOIL DISRUPTION to preserve the soil's natural layering. Soil should not be turned over by hand, by rototiller, or by plow. Even when setting transplants, shrubs, and trees in the ground, take care not to disrupt the natural layering of the soil any more than necessary.

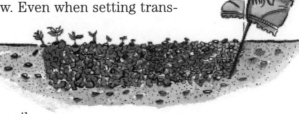

Dormant weed seeds awaken, over time, once tillage exposes them to light and air.

2. PROTECT THE SOIL SURFACE with some sort of covering to temper the effects of hot sun and raindrops on the surface and to smother small weed seedlings. What to use depends on the availability of various materials, your style of garden, and the kinds of plants

Night Tillage

Agricultural researchers have been able to reduce the sprouting of weed seeds by tilling at night instead of by day. Weeds affected were broadleaf annuals such as lamb's-quarters, pigweed, smartweed, and ragweed. These small seeds don't have enough reserves to support growth for long in dark soil, and so would be expected to need light for germination.

But hold off donning your military-issue night-vision goggles and going out to rototill tonight. Seeds of grasses and large-seeded broadleaf weeds do sprout well following cultivation in light *or* darkness; they're only waiting for a breath of air to awaken them.

If you do choose to till at night, be careful about using *any* light, even a flashlight, because even short bursts of light can induce germination in those small-seeded annuals. Also, avoid moonlit nights because the silvery glow might be bright enough to induce sprouting of light-sensitive seeds brought to the surface.

you grow. In some situations, living plants might offer the needed protection.

3. AVOID SOIL COMPACTION by keeping off planted areas with feet, wheelbarrows, garden carts, and tractors. This is done by designating separate areas for plants and for traffic. The design of trafficked areas (usually paths) varies with the design of the garden and the kind of traffic expected.

4. USE DRIP IRRIGATION. Watering is not always needed, but when it is required regularly, drip is the way to go. Drip irrigation quenches plants' thirst at a rate close to their actual needs. It pinpoints the water where it's needed, instead of wastefully wetting paths and weeds in unplanted areas.

More on the details and wrinkles of Weedless Gardening later on. For now, lest the idea of spending only a few minutes per week weeding is not enough to convince you to adopt this system, an enumeration of other benefits likely will.

The Benefits: Let Us Count the Ways

The most obvious appeal of Weedless Gardening is dispensing with the annual ritual of turning over soil. No more wrestling a rototiller up and down garden rows. No more making arrangements for someone to plow. Gone are the repeated thuds of your garden spade coming up against rocks in rocky soil. Forget about needing that "iron back, with a hinge in it," suggested as the ideal anatomy for a gardener by Charles Dudley Warner in *My Summer in a Garden* (1870).

Dispensing with digging also means being able to get plants and seeds into the ground sooner. One reason for digging in spring is to kill existing vegetation, be it weeds, a deliberately planted cover crop, or

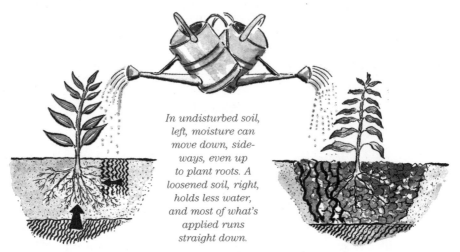

In undisturbed soil, left, moisture can move down, sideways, even up to plant roots. A loosened soil, right, holds less water, and most of what's applied runs straight down.

(for a new garden) lawn grass. The digging is followed by a burst of biological activity in the soil as bacteria and fungi, fueled by a shot of air, gobble up chopped-up roots, stems, and leaves. This is too much commotion for seeds and small plants, so planting must be delayed for a couple of weeks until microbial activity settles down. Then another run over the ground is sometimes needed to further break up the soil and plants, causing a delay of another week or two.

Not having to dig the soil in spring also means not having to delay planting because of wet soil. Digging a wet clay soil transforms it into a compact material better suited for sculpture than plant growth. The frustration is twofold: Planting is delayed until the soil is dry enough to dig; and after planting, you must wait for rain to get seeds and plants growing. Skip the digging and all that's needed in spring is to drop seeds or nestle plants into the ground.

Leaving soil undisturbed in spring even helps plants quench their thirst later in the season. Earthworms, roots of various dimensions, even the action of freezing and thawing all work together to create interconnecting large and small pores within which air and water move and new roots grow. Gravity quickly empties large channels of excess water, drawing air in, yet small pores of capillary dimensions cling to water against the pull of gravity. As long as these pores stay intact, water can move within them—down, sideways, even up—to replace water that nearby roots drink in.

Another benefit of not turning the soil is that organic materials remain on the surface. There, they can provide a soft landing for rain-drops, allowing moisture to soak in rather than run off and water your lawn or your neighbor's garden. Organic materials at the soil's surface also temper the effects of winter's cold and the sun's heat, and slow water evaporation. If you mix organic materials into the soil or bury them down deep, they cannot do their job of protecting the soil surface.

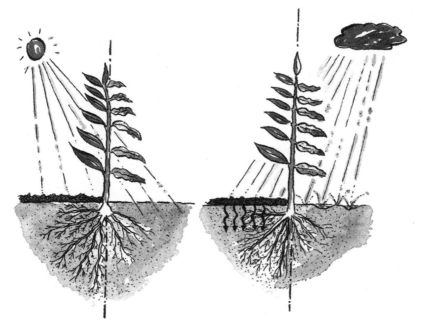

Organic matter best does its job of protecting the soil from pelting rain and hot sun if left on the surface.

Not tilling also avoids creating a plowpan, a hardened layer within the soil that impedes drainage. Plowpans form when rototillers or plows are used at the same depth season after season, causing soil compaction just beneath the depth of tillage.

Perhaps the greatest benefit of leaving the soil undisturbed is that it preserves organic matter, including humus, the touchstone of any great garden soil. Digging, rototilling, or plowing puts such a shot of oxygen into the soil that microbial activity is stimulated to the point of burning up organic matter too rapidly. It literally disappears into thin air, most of it becoming carbon dioxide and water vapor.

It's not that these microbes should starve. After all, plant foods are released and a healthy microbial population is supported only as

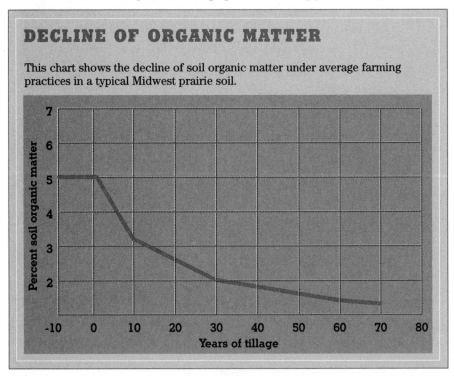

DECLINE OF ORGANIC MATTER

This chart shows the decline of soil organic matter under average farming practices in a typical Midwest prairie soil.

As If Once Were Not Enough

A tradition that deserves to die is that of deliberately burying organic materials in the soil to facilitate water drainage. A plow can do this, as can a strong back and a shovel, by double-digging. As if one digging were not enough, double-digging entails digging out a trench, mixing organic materials in the bottom of that trench, then turning over adjacent soil into the trench—thus creating another trench that is treated the same way. And so on across the garden. Burying organic materials is not only a waste of time, but the effect is actually the opposite of what is intended. A water table (or perched water table) actually develops atop the drastic change in soil porosity created by the wad of buried organic materials.

organic matter is gobbled up. Problems arise, though, when organic matter is burned too fast, which happens when soils are tilled. In untilled soils topped with organic materials, the materials are consumed at a rate that doesn't outstrip the rate at which they are replenished.

Do Plants Like It?

All the information offered so far has sung the praises of Weedless Gardening for you, me, and the soil, but what about the plants? How do delphiniums, rosebushes, and bean and tomato plants feel about growing in soil that is never turned over or stirred up, yet is perpetually blanketed with compost, wood chips, or some other organic mulch? The answer is, they like it.

After all, an undisturbed soil blanketed with organic mulch becomes increasingly rich in humus, one by-product of the decomposition of organic matter. Humus is not a single compound but a witches' brew of stuff beneficial to plants. It is to plants what a vitamin-rich salad is to you and me—not

Nature's Richest Soils

The earth's richest agricultural soils—the American prairie, the Argentine pampa, the Russian steppe, and the African veldt—owe their richness to an accumulation of relatively large amounts of organic matter. These soils are classified as mollisols, derived from the word *mollis,* Latin for "soft," which highlights one of their qualities.

Mollisols are formed where the natural vegetation is grassland. At the end of each season, these grasses deposit the year's accumulation of leaves and stems on the ground's surface. Just below the surface, a tightly bundled network of roots makes its contribution to soil organic matter. A prairie and a forest have similar amounts of organic matter, on the order of about 150 tons per acre. In the forest, though, more than half that organic matter is standing timber. In the prairie, just about all the organic matter is in and on the ground.

Mollisols can take hundreds or thousands of years to develop naturally, depending on the nature of the underlying rock, the climate, and the vegetation. "Breaking the prairie" was an apt expression for what it took to get a plow through that tight bundle of roots in the 1800s. Unfortunately, stirring up the soil of the American prairies quickly burned up centuries of accumulated organic matter; within 60 years, more than a third of the humus had been lost. That loss of organic matter (one benefit of which is to stabilize soil against wind and water erosion) was dramatically demonstrated when it was coupled with a few years of drought to create the Dust Bowls of the 1930s.

a concentrated food, but one offering a wide spectrum of nutrients and other good things. (In addition to the nutrients coming from the humus itself, it also contains substances that help nutrients already in the soil become more accessible to plants.) Humus also serves as the bulk in a plant's "diet," fluffing up soil with air and at the same time holding water like a sponge. Humus even helps plants fight off pests with protective compounds, and by supporting friendly microorganisms that fend off pathogens.

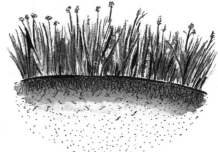

Nature nourishes her soils from the top down—in the forest with falling leaves, and in prairie and meadow with old leaves, stems, and roots.

Conventional wisdom would have us mixing humus-rich materials deep into the soil "where the roots are," or so the logic goes. However, the bulk of a plant's feeder roots, whether the plant is a mighty oak or a midget marigold, actually lie near the surface of the soil. Roots need air to function, and they do their best work in the well-aerated surface layers. There, roots can rub shoulders with the numerous beneficial soil microorganisms that thrive where air and organic "fuels" are most abundant.

After all, for millions of years Nature has been creating soils in just this way, from the top down. Leaf litter drops on the surface of the ground, then gradually decomposes to form humus, some benefits of which are carried down into the soil over time. Old roots similarly decompose and make their contribution to humus.

The difference between natural soils, which require hundreds of years to develop, and our backyards is that we don't have to rely only

Earthworms: Nature's Tillers

Charles Darwin was sufficiently enamored with earthworms to spend nights with them in an English pasture. Up to the time of his studies, which culminated in 1896 with the publication of *The Formation of Vegetable Mould Through the Action of Worms*, these creatures had been thought detrimental to gardening and farming.

Today everyone knows that worms are good for gardens. As organic matter and soil pass through earthworms' guts, nutrients are put in a form more readily absorbed by plant roots. Channels left by earthworms help break up the soil and provide spaces in which roots, water, and air can pass. The thousands of such channels in a square yard of soil is less surprising when you realize that 500 worms might live there.

In creating channels, worms are Nature's plow, moving materials both up from below and down from above. Darwin estimated that worms turn over the top 6 inches of soil every 20 years and wrote: "The plow is one of the most ancient and most valuable of man's inventions; but long before he existed the land was in fact regularly plowed by earthworms."

The numbers of earthworms and how much good they do vary with location and environment. Not all regions are equally endowed with the most desirable of countless earthworm species—they had to be imported into Australia to help manage the growing accumulation of manure from feedlots. (Indigenous species were only capable of dealing with lesser amounts of kangaroo waste.) And earthworms in the northern part of the United States are virtually all immigrants from Europe, inadvertently brought over by white settlers. These worms colonized ground left wormless after the last glaciers left the region about 18,000 years ago.

Great garden soils have earthworms in them, but adding worms will not make a garden soil great. You need to provide conditions under which worms thrive. First, they like plenty of organic materials to eat, preferably applied as a surface mulch. Second, they need undisturbed soil, mostly because tilling or otherwise disturbing the soil quickly burns up organic matter.

on leaves, stems, and roots of resident plants for soil building. We can haul in materials such as wood chips, manure from a nearby farm, and autumn leaves our neighbors just raked up. We can also speed up humus formation by building compost piles.

Why Do We Dig?

When asked why they turn over the soil, many farmers or gardeners will simply respond, "Because." People have turned their soil, or attempted to, since the dawn of civilization.

A more thoughtful rationale for turning the soil is to facilitate aeration. But soils generally need aeration only because they've been compacted. And what causes soil compaction? People tromping on it, day after day, throughout the season (6 to 10 pounds of pressure per square inch from each footstep), and driving over it with tractors and rototillers. Compaction can be avoided by not driving or walking on the soil in the first place—not an impractical solution if separate areas are permanently set aside for plants and for traffic. Note that even sticky clay soils, the kinds most easily compacted, are not naturally barren of plants except where they become thoroughfares.

Churning the soil is also touted as useful for clearing the ground of weeds, but remember that this benefit is short-lived. Exsisting weeds are killed, but the ground remains clear only until once-buried weed seeds sprout. Better to keep weed seeds buried and asleep in the first place.

Admittedly, there is some satisfaction that comes from tilling the soil. You get to sweat a little (or a lot, depending on your equipment); you get to thoroughly erase last year's mistakes (even 3-foot-tall weeds); and when finished, you get to look out upon an expanse of smoothed, dark brown soil. As Robert Penn Warren put it in *Meet Me in the Green Glen:* "He liked the picture of himself sitting on the tractor and it shining with new paint. He could feel the sense of power as the plowshares sliced solidly through the earth and left it folded behind him, open and shining in the sun with the polish left by the sharp steel."

If you cannot restrain yourself from tilling the soil, I suggest setting aside an area (a small one) where you can dig to your heart's content. You might even want to plant it. And weed it, of course. Personally, I find that the digging associated with periodically dividing perennial flowers and shoveling compost sufficiently satisfies my urge to slide a shovel into soft earth and turn it over.

CHAPTER TWO

In the Beginning: Readying the Ground for a First-Time Planting

O ne of the great appeals of Weedless Gardening is the ease and speed with which you can get plants up and growing. The steps involved are simplicity itself, applicable to any planting, be it vegetables, flowers, shrubs, vines, or trees.

Preparing a garden the weedless way involves no more than sprinkling fertilizer over a potential planting area, knocking or mowing down existing vegetation, blanketing the ground with paper, and covering it with organic material. Variations arise in the layout of different plantings and in choices of what organic covering (compost, wood chips, straw, etc.) works best for you and the plants.

This chapter will detail how to ready all types of ground for Weedless Gardening. Special accommodations for sites that are too wet or too rocky, or where the soil acidity needs drastic change, accompany the basic steps. If you're just giving over part of your lawn—your lush, healthy lawn—to a new bed of vegetables or flowers, the proce-dure entails so little time and effort that you could plant the same morning.

Eliminating Any Existing Vegetation

Your proposed planting site might be an established, weed-free garden due for a makeover, but more likely it is awash with plants, vegetation that might be a hayfield or meadow, a lawn or weeds. No planting can be done until the existing vegetation is done away with.

The first step when preparing a new garden site is to fertilize. For every 100 square feet of planted area, spread 6 cups of any complete fertilizer that contains about 5 percent nitrogen. Adjust the application rate accordingly if your fertilizer has a greater or lesser percentage of nitrogen. (For example, my newest vegetable plot received 4 cups per 100 square feet of soybean meal, which is 7 percent nitrogen, along with some wood ash and rock phosphate for potassium and phospho-rus, respectively.) Later, we'll examine various kinds of fertilizers that might be used for maintaining a planting.

After fertilizing, flatten existing vegetation: Stamp it down with your booted foot, cut it down with a machete, sickle, or scythe, or mow it with

Begin site preparation by mowing or otherwise knocking down existing vegetation.

your lawnmower—whatever it takes to lay all the plants flat on the ground. A combination of methods (such as stamping followed by close mowing) often works best to get vegetation as low and as smooth over the ground as possible.

A paper blanket—newspaper, here—smothers existing vegetation to prevent resprouting. Wetted, the paper stays in place.

Power mowing is not necessary, but it will chop vegetation and speed its decomposition.

The vegetation is now down but not dead. The roots are still alive, ready to sprout new stems and leaves. The way to prevent resprouting is by smothering the plants beneath a temporary, impenetrable blanket that shades the new leaves trying to emerge. The roots will eventually starve.

Paper is the perfect material for this gruesome-sounding job. It eventually decomposes, but the paper is only needed for the short while it takes to kill existing plants. It is also readily available and usually cheap or free—a perfect use for that old pile of newspapers you were waiting to recycle. If you don't have enough newspaper yourself, neighbors will be

Cover the paper with organic materials—here, in my vegetable garden, with wood chips in the paths and compost in the beds—and then plant.

A Permanent Solution to Weeds?

Black plastic sheeting sold as mulch appears, at first blush, to be a cure-all for weed problems. Lay it on the ground, cut holes only where you will set plants, and weeds die from lack of light.

But problems arise. An impermeable sheet of plastic over the ground can leave plant roots and soil microorganisms gasping for air. Roots of plants set in the openings made in the plastic might develop even greater breathing problems when all the water falling on the plastic is channeled into those openings. And the plastic eventually starts to tear and break apart, which creates a general mess.

Geotextiles, which are synthetic fabrics resistant to tearing and having many small holes that allow air and water to penetrate the soil, have been offered as an alternative to black plastic. Both black plastic and geotextiles are widely used by farmers, gardeners, and landscapers.

If you don't like the way these synthetic mulches look—surely the case when they are used in landscaping—you can cover them. Wood chips look natural and are widely used for this purpose. And anyway, geotextiles need a thin cover of something to shade out the minimal light that makes its way though the tiny holes.

But problems arise again. If you cover an area with black plastic or geotextiles and expect to do nothing more, you'll find that plenty of weeds eventually trot in, their roots growing into that cover of wood chips. In time, the chips or other covering starts to move, exposing the plastic or geotextile beneath—not a pretty sight.

Furthermore, even if black plastic or geotextiles don't do their jobs forever, they'll be in the soil that long, or almost so. Try to make over the landscape in the future, and you'll be wrestling with and cutting geotextiles or collecting scraps of black plastic. Embedding a permanent, synthetic blanket in the ground also shows a fundamental disrespect for the soil.

happy enough to share it or you can get more from recycling centers. An alternative to newspaper is landscape barrier paper or building paper (such as gray rosin paper, which is undyed and made from recycled newspaper). Any basic paper will do, but avoid those with colored inks.

Spread the paper blanket over the whole planting area. A four-layer thickness of newspaper or a single layer of landscape barrier paper or building paper will generally do the job, but you may have to adjust the number of layers somewhat according to how vigorously you expect existing vegetation to resprout. In a hayfield of vigorous plants covered in early spring—a time when roots are packed with stored energy in anticipation of the upcoming growing season—a thicker layer will be needed. On the other hand, a sorry patch of lawn will quickly expire beneath less than four layers of newspaper (but there's no harm in using that much anyway). Make sure to overlap the edges of the paper or sprouts will surely wend their way up to light. Wet the paper to keep it in place as you lay it down. This will also allow roots from your first planting to easily grow down into and through it.

A Suitable Mulch

To keep your carefully laid paper from just blowing away or curling up and letting weeds peek through, cover it with mulch. If you're going to be planting seeds or small transplants, the paper also needs to be covered deep enough to plant in without making holes in it (except for tree and shrub transplants). And the paper needs to be covered to keep it moist, which starts it on the road

How Much Mulch?

To cover a 100-square-foot area 1 inch deep requires ⅓ cubic yard of mulching material.

MULCH GUIDE

Kind of Mulch	Availability	Characteristics
Bark chips	*Purchase in bags*	Weed-free; long-lasting; moderately good at smothering small weeds; not as good at conserving moisture as most other mulches; pretty to some people
Compost	*Purchase or make your own*	Weed-free if properly made; smorgasboard of plant foods; helps prevent diseases
Grass clippings	*Whenever you or your neighbors mow your lawn;* do not *use clippings from lawns treated with weed killers*	Usually weed-free; high in nitrogen; thick layers will heat up, so apply no more then 1–2" thick and not near stems of young plants; very good at smothering weed seedlings
Hay	*Cut your own, collect along roadsides, or buy in bales*	Good at smothering weeds but contains weed seeds; better used in feeding and/or enclosing compost pile; salt hay is gathered from marshes and so will not bring weeds to your garden
Hulls and shells	*Bagged for purchase, perhaps free where grown or processed*	Includes hulls and shells of peanuts, buckwheat, cocoa bean, and rice; weed-free and fairly rich in nutrients; best for smothering weed seedlings or keeping weeds out of weed-free areas; attractive in formal or informal gardens; longevity varies
Leaves	*Free for the raking; also from neighbors*	Weed-free except for occasional tree seeds; good at smothering weeds; holds in soil moisture very well; tends to blow, especially, when dry or at exposed sites
Peat moss	*Purchase in bags*	Weed-free; poor in nutrients; attractive; tends to blow when dry, and is hard to re-wet; repels water when dry

KIND OF MULCH	AVAILABILITY	CHARACTERISTICS
Pine needles	*Rake your own (although your pines would like them left in place); can be bought in some areas*	Weed-free; long-lasting; moderately good at smothering weeds; pretty; don't worry about pH effects
Sawdust	*Usually free, but can be purchased by the truckload*	Weed-free; long-lasting; good at smothering weed seedlings; avoid sawdust from pressure-treated or painted wood
Seaweed	*Often collected or dumped for free*	Weed-free; nutrient rich; not long-lasting; excellent at smothering weeds when fresh
Stone	*Usually purchased, of various rock in various colors*	Weed-free and essentially nutrient-free; mostly for paths, and perhaps around cacti and other succulents; lasts almost forever but needs periodic weeding by raking or plucking
Straw	*Purchase baled*	Should be weed-free; replenish annually; very good at smothering weeds and holding soil moisture
Wood chips	*Purchase or obtain free by the truckload*	Weed-free; moderately long-lasting; good at smothering weeds

to decomposition and lets roots of seeds and small transplants grow down into and through it (even before it decomposes). Finally, covering the paper makes things prettier.

Any mulch used for covering the paper must be free of weed seeds or pieces of roots and stems that might regrow. This makes a mulch of hay or uncomposted weeds unsuitable. What to cover the paper with depends on what you're going to do with a particular area, what you have on hand, and how you want the ground to look.

Lay out beds and paths before covering the paper. Stakes and strings or a sprinkling of dark soil or compost helps delineate these areas as they're prepared. (See Chapters Five and Six for suggested vegetable and flower garden layouts.) Once boundaries are staked out, an easy way to lay down a crisp, straight line of material is by setting an 8- or 10-foot-long 2" × 4" board on edge at one boundary. Apply mulching material right up to and against the board, then move it into position for other boundaries. Lay material down a shovelful or pitch-forkful at a time where beds and paths are curved.

Straw-Bale Culture

Straw-bale culture of vegetables originated in Europe out of a need to grow plants where diseases had built up in greenhouse soils. The idea is to set a bale of straw on the ground and grow a plant right in the bale. This is done by poking a transplant into a hole gouged in the top of the bale, and sprinkling some fertilizer on it. Given adequate water and nutrients, the plant roots grow throughout the bale, hardly realizing that they're not in real soil. There's no reason why this method could not be used to start a small garden anywhere. Put some paper down on the ground and create mulched paths between the bales.

A number of mulching materials can be used to cover paths. More or less permanent mulches include gravel, flagstone, crushed oyster shells, and bricks. Organic materials typically used include wood chips, straw, sawdust, leaves, and pine needles. A living option for paths is lawn grass, which you can plant or, if present already, simply leave in place uncovered when you ready the site for planting. Make sure the grass is a noninvasive sort, then keep it mowed and edged. Among quirkier path coverings are old carpet pads (horsehair ones are biodegradable) and wooden planks.

Any of the aforementioned weed-free, organic materials

How High Are My Beds?

Say "bed planting" and most gardeners quickly think "raised beds." Raised beds have their place in gardening as a way of dealing with wet soils. They're also justified on rocky ledges where soil is almost nonexistent. (And a tall friend once pointed out that raised beds bring the ground closer to him.)

Except in special circumstances, however, I don't recommend raised beds. In addition to the effort and soil disruption necessary to create them, raised beds tend to dry out quickly, and the higher and narrower they are, the quicker they dry out.

If raised beds have their place in gardening, so do the other extreme— sunken beds. They've been used by traditional gardeners in arid Mexico, New Mexico, and West Africa to capture and conserve water. In this method, soil excavated from beds creates a waffle pattern of walkways crisscrossing lush, sunken patches of vegetation.

In arid climates, sunken beds collect rainwater and shield young plants from drying winds.

The advantages of sunken beds in arid climates are twofold: First, seedlings and other low-growing plants within the beds are spared the full force of drying winds so they lose less moisture; and second, rainwater is channeled into the low-lying beds and contained there until absorbed by the soil.

(wood chips, straw, sawdust, leaves, pine needles) are also suitable for covering planting areas. Compost also needs to be added to this list— it's the material of choice for especially hungry plants and wherever you are going to plant seeds.

Any organic materials, whether used to cover planting or walking areas, should be applied 1 to 3 inches deep. Using different materials in beds and paths makes it obvious where to walk, and can lend some artistry to a garden. The Mulch Guide on pages 24–25 lists some of the most common mulching materials.

Edges

Garden edges serve as aesthetic transitions and as barriers. Weeds, including certain grasses, incessantly try to elbow their way into a planted area (even in Weedless Gardens) at the edges. The richer the soil, the greater their efforts, so yours must be equally vigilant.

One way to ease your labors in dealing with encroaching weeds is to minimize the number of edges by massing plants together. Four rose-bushes, each planted in the center of its own 3-foot-diameter bed, result in about 36 feet of edging. A single bed containing the same four roses, still with 3 feet of bare soil surrounding each plant, will have only 24 feet of edging.

Over time, gardeners have come up with numerous ways to foil plants at the edges of plantings. Border patrol might entail nothing more elaborate than donning a pair of gloves, dropping to your knees, and ripping out interlopers. This method works fine (and is quite satisfying in the soft soil where ground ivy spills over and tries to gain footing in my bed of currants, Nanking cherries, and saskatoons mulched thickly with wood chips).

One traditional way to maintain crisp edges is by hand-pulling weeds.

Any physical method that grinds, chops, or otherwise mutilates encroaching plants at the garden edge is also effective if done frequently enough, which means every few weeks. A hoe is the simplest implement. Years ago, when I still owned a rototiller but no longer tilled, I would start the machine up a few times during the season for a pass around the outside edge of my vegetable garden. It created an effective Maginot Line for weeds. (Eventually, I tired of seeing bare soil there, and opted to mulch and plant the area instead.) Another powered contrivance, the lawn edger, cuts a vertical strip in the ground. My efforts with this machine resulted in an unpleasant face full of dirt.

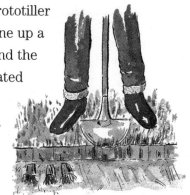

A half-moon edger keeps a neat borderline for a planted area.

And finally, there's the traditional half-moon-shaped lawn edger. The going is slow with this tool—each step advances you only another 9 inches around the garden's perimeter. But the work is satisfyingly quiet and leaves a crisp edge.

Mechanical barriers, another edging option, confront plant interlopers with an impasse through which they cannot grow. Bricks, stone walls, and railroad ties can all be effectively integrated into the overall design of a garden. Aside from occasional checks for stray plants trying to hurdle the barrier, these edgings require no regular maintenance. They are particularly effective for creating raised beds because then errant weeds have to not only cross a barrier, but also climb it. For ground-level beds, though, be careful of weeds that insinuate themselves between adjacent bricks, stones, or railroad ties—they are particularly hard to remove.

Barriers of metal or plastic are

A powered edger mechanizes the job of the half-moon edger—in theory.

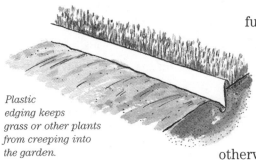

Plastic edging keeps grass or other plants from creeping into the garden.

functional but not particularly attractive. They also need some sort of anchor to keep them embedded in place where annual freezing and thawing of soil would otherwise lift them out.

Concrete cinder blocks laid on their sides slightly above soil level (so one side of the mower wheels can roll on them) make a very effective mechanical barrier. At first this might not seem like a particularly attractive choice for edging, but the character of the concrete surface improves with age as a thin patina of green algae and mosses mellows the surface.

Another type of edging, especially suitable for informal gardens, are plants that can stand up to grass and other invaders. Such plants need to be dense-growing and/or somewhat invasive in their own right. A dense mat of creeping thyme can form a low, smooth transition between a mowed area and taller-growing plants. Wormwood is a perennial that starts growth early in the spring and shades out competing plants. Periwinkle, pachysandra, bishop's weed, hosta, English ivy, and potentilla are other candidates. Living edges defined by these plants need only occasional weeding, but should be monitored against becoming garden weeds themselves. An ideal edging plant is not so aggressive that it invades the garden, but is strong enough to fight back lawn grass.

Brick is both a functional and decorative edging.

Exceptions to Top-Down Beginnings

Although Weedless Gardening techniques fit every garden situation, there is the rare site that might require soil disruption or (shudder at the thought) a thorough, initial digging or rototilling. Mind you, this is a one-time disruption of the soil. Afterward, basic Weedless Gardening practices apply.

Acid Balance

Digging becomes necessary when the soil acidity (the pH) is way out of whack for the plants you want to grow. Soil acidity needs to be in the proper range for roots to effectively absorb nutrients and for beneficial microorganisms to thrive. Most garden plants enjoy slightly acidic soil, with a pH of 6 to 7. Heath plants such as blueberry, azalea, rhododendron, heather, and of course heath itself are notable exceptions, thriving only in very acidic soils with a pH of 4 to 5.

Simply looking at your soil can give you an idea of its acidity. You'll often find cinquefoil, coltsfoot, hawkweed, horsetail, mullein, stinging nettle, plantain, sorrel, blueberry, mountain laurel, hemlock, and/or wild strawberry growing in acidic soils. Bellflower, campion, Queen Anne's lace, black henbane, and pennycress are common denizens of alkaline soils.

A more exact way to determine your soil's acidity is with a soil test (see page 186 for more information about sampling and soil testing).

Ground limestone (lime) or sulfur, used to make soil less or more acidic respectively, works its way through the soil slowly. If a radical and quick change in acidity is needed, spread the required amount of either material on top of the ground, then thoroughly mix it into the top 6 to 12 inches of soil.

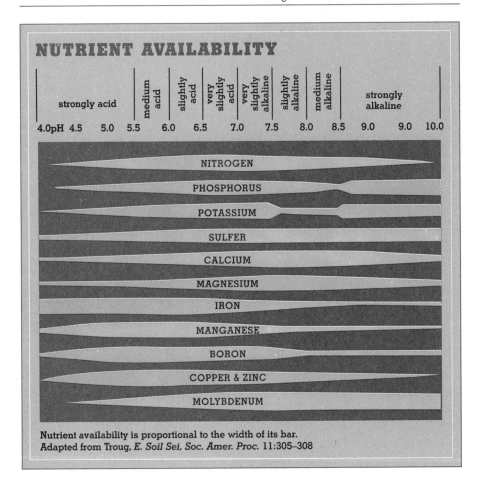

NUTRIENT AVAILABILITY

Nutrient availability is proportional to the width of its bar.
Adapted from Troug, E. Soil Sei, Soc. Amer. Proc. 11:305–308

Rocky Beginnings

Places where bedrock comes to the surface have little or no natural soil. Alpine plants nestled in dirt-filled crevices look right at home here, but more soil is needed if you want to plant a tree, or have a vegetable garden or flower bed. Construct enclosures a foot or more high—stone would be a natural choice—to enclose planting beds, then fill the beds almost to the top with some well-drained soil such as sand or loam.

Do not use a soil too rich in organic matter or the soil level will sink as the organic matter oxidizes. Spread 6 cups per 100 square feet of some fertilizer containing 5 percent nitrogen (or the equivalent of any fertilizer to give the same rate of nitrogen) on top of the soil. Finally, add organic matter such as compost, wood chips, or straw, putting it where Nature does—on top of the soil. A 1- to 2-inch layer will do.

Slurpy Soil

Overly wet soil is a common complaint among gardeners and is a condition to avoid or cor-

This tree's roots find a home in a soil bed created atop bedrock.

rect unless the plan is to grow plants that enjoy a boggy or flooded environment. Recent interest in native plants has widened the spectrum of what we grow to include many plants whose natural habitats are bogs or ponds, but most traditional garden plants demand well-drained soil. One option worth considering, if a soil is unsuitably wet, is choosing another site for planting altogether.

• **ASSESSMENT:** You know drainage of a piece of ground is poor if you see water. The presence of wetland plants such as purple loosestrife, yellow flag, cardinal flower, buttercup, horsetail, Joe-Pye weed, smartweed, sedges, buttonbush, winterberry, rhodora, and cattails is another indication. But don't be led astray by soil wet on just one day, or by one or two wetland plants that are struggling in soil that is actually well drained.

Digging a hole is the most direct way to assess drainage if you factor into your soil evaluation recent weather conditions like rain and time of year (even when not frozen, soils drain more slowly in cold weather than in warm). Dig the hole wide enough to accommodate a large (perhaps 1-quart) can. Cut the top and bottom off the can, then press it into the soil at the bottom of the hole so that water cannot run out its bottom edge. Fill the can with water and let it sit until all

A "can test" quantitatively assesses soil drainage.

the water drains out the bottom into the soil. Then fill the can with water again, and this time measure how fast the level drops. Drainage is poor if the water level drops any slower than 1 inch per hour.

• CAUSES AND CURES FOR WETNESS: Abundant clay is one cause for a soil that's too wet. Soil rich in clay is sticky when wet and hard when dry. Although many clay soils need no special treatment, there are those so goopy when wet and so rock hard when dry that an initial digging is called for.

One way to loosen up clay soil is by mixing in abundant organic matter, which clumps the small clay particles into larger units with correspondingly larger spaces (for air) between them. Many organic materials will suffice, but peat moss or sawdust is ideal for this particular situation. The small particles mingle intimately with the clay, and both materials decay slowly. (Sawdust also has the advantage of being either cheap or free. Look in the Yellow Pages under "Sawmills," "Cabinet Makers," "Millwork," and "Woodworking." Avoid sawdust containing pressure-treated or painted wood.)

When the soil is moist—that is neither very wet nor very dry—spread a 6-inch layer of sawdust or peat moss on top of the area slated for planting. A 6-inch layer works out to about 2 cubic yards per 100 square feet. Because peat moss or sawdust makes the soil temporarily more acidic, add limestone at the rate of 60 pounds per 100 square feet—unless you actually want to make the soil more acidic. For sawdust, add some extra nitrogen fertilizer because soil microorganisms temporarily borrow nitrogen from the soil to decompose that sawdust at the expense of plants. Spread 100 pounds of some fertilizer containing 10 percent nitrogen on top of the sawdust (adjust the fertilizer rate accordingly if you use one having more or less than 10 percent nitrogen).

Go ahead and mix the peat moss or sawdust into the top foot or so of soil. Do it thoroughly, spurred by the realization that you'll never have to dig or till the ground again. (And of course, you'll never again set foot on it either.)

Another situation that calls for a one-time digging is clay soil that drains poorly because it's high in sodium. Such soils are prevalent in drier regions of the American West. Sodium prevents the clumping of small clay particles into larger units, a condition remedied by exchanging sodium for calcium, usually in the form of gypsum. Acidity resulting from application of sulfur or iron sulfate can dissolve calcium carbonate in soils to release calcium and produce the same effect.

Thoroughly mix the gypsum, sulfur, or iron sulfate into the top half-foot or so of soil, then follow the digging with a heavy application of water to leach out the sodium. A soil test for sodium and a recommendation from your local Cooperative Extension Service will tell you how much material to apply. In the case of gypsum, common applications are on the order of 20 pounds per 100 square feet.

A soil that stays consistently wet could also be the result of a shallow water table. You know the water table is shallow if you see standing water on the ground for much or all of the year, or if you dig a hole and the water never drains.

One way to get plant roots out of the water is to simply lower the water table by draining the water away to lower ground either in open ditches or in buried, perforated plastic pipes. (The Natural Resource Soil Conservation Service provides technical assistance for drainage projects.) The more clay in the soil, the more closely spaced ditches or pipes need to be in order to draw off the water.

A drainage ditch does not have to be large. A shovel's width is sufficient breadth for a garden. The deeper the ditch, the greater the depth of well-aerated soil that results, so dig at least 18 inches deep. A gradual slope along the length of any ditch, about a half-foot per 100 feet, keeps the water flowing downhill.

A high-water table is lowered either by drainage "tile" (top) or by ditches (bottom).

Ditches crisscrossing your garden need not be either an eyesore or an inconvenience. I once saw a garden where flat stones were used to line ditches and to serve as bridges across ditches that intersected paths. The whole system created an elegant water feature, similar in effect to that of a classic Persian garden. (In the latter case, however, the long, narrow waterways were used to bring water to the plants.)

Perforated pipe buried beneath

the ground drains water away without changing a site's appearance. Four-inch-diameter black plastic drainage pipes (available at home- and building-supply stores) can be laid in pre-dug trenches. Cover the pipes with some fabric or paper to keep out dirt, then add a layer of gravel and backfill the soil. A screen at the outlet end of the pipe keeps out curious animals.

Planting on a mound raises this tree's roots above the water table.

Instead of lowering the water table to rescue roots, you can get them out of the water by raising them above the water table. Construct enclosures for planting beds and fill them as you would with rocky soil (see page 33). When raising the soil level to improve drainage for new individual trees, shrubs, or vines, wide mounds are more appropriate than beds.

Just as a garden crisscrossed with stone-lined ditches can carry you on a magic carpet to ancient Persia, a pattern of raised beds, as well as the materials used for their sides and the paths between them, might transport your garden to another time, another place. That time and place might be medieval Europe if the edgings are of sawn timbers and the paths of beige pea-gravel. Line the beds with rough-cut logs and lay straw or crushed oyster shells in the paths, and you might instead imagine hitching your horse to a post outside this shadow of a Colonial American garden. Or build raised beds and ditches at the same time,

WORKSHEET FOR BEGINNING A GARDEN/PLANTING

MY GARDEN/PLANTINGS
VEGETABLE GARDEN

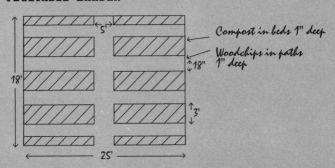

Compost in beds 1" deep

Woodchips in paths 1" deep

MATERIAL NEEDED	SOURCE(S)	TOTAL AREA, SQ. FT.[1]	AMOUNT NEEDED[2]
Newspaper	Recycled	450	450 sq. ft.
Soybean meal	Agway	450	27 cups
Wood chips	Three Bros. Tree Service	210	0.7 cu. yd.
Compost	Homemade	240	0.8 cu. yd.

CHESTNUT TREES

MATERIAL NEEDED	SOURCE(S)	TOTAL AREA, SQ. FT.[1]	AMOUNT NEEDED[2]
Wood chips	Three Bros. Tree Service	81	0.8 yd.[3]

[1] TOTAL AREA = sum of length × width of each rectangular area
or
= 3 × radius × radius for each circular area
[2] FERTILIZER (about 5% nitrogen) NEEDED = 0.06 cups × total area
MULCH (compost, wood chips, etc.) NEEDED = 0.0033 × total areas × depth (inches)

YOUR GARDEN/PLANTINGS

_____ GARDEN

MATERIAL NEEDED	SOURCE(s)	TOTAL AREA, SQ. FT.[1]	AMOUNT NEEDED[2]

_____ TREES

MATERIAL NEEDED	SOURCE(s)	TOTAL AREA, SQ. FT.[1]	AMOUNT NEEDED[2]

emulating those old-time gardeners of Xochimilco. Plant plenty of marigolds, a favorite flower in Xochimilco, to lend authenticity to such a garden, and have a boat ready to ply the paths if they are, indeed, permanently water-filled ditches.

Hardpan

The presence of a hardpan—a hardened layer within the soil through which roots and water penetrate only slowly—might require a one-time digging. Pans form naturally in soils where certain minerals or types of clay particles accumulate and cement themselves together. They can also result from traffic on the ground, or from repeated tillage to the same depth. Slow drainage is a symptom of a hardpan. Dig a hole and you may be able to see or feel a layer of hardened material. Your neighbors or the Natural Resource Soil Conservation Service might be able to tell you if hardpan soils are prevalent in your area.

Time and deep-rooted plants can eventually break up a pan, but a quicker way is to use a long-bladed spade, garden fork, or rototiller. Turning the soil over is not as important as breaking through the hardened layer in this case. Once you have broken up the pan, the new environment associated with cultivated plants—what you add to the soil, what you grow, and keeping traffic off the surface—should eliminate the need for ever again disrupting it with spade, garden fork, or tiller.

CHAPTER THREE

Through the Year in the Weedless Garden

Regular maintenance goes a long way in getting the Weedless Garden to almost care for itself. What's needed on a more or less regular basis is cleaning up and mulching—all done, of course, from the top down. At times, you might also opt to plant a cover crop to smother weeds and improve the soil. And yes, occasional light weeding is necessary.

Depending on the site, the plants, and how you garden, not all facets of Weedless Garden maintenance are needed in every garden, every year. The total time spent doing any or even all of these tasks is truly minimal—as attested to by the boredom of my daughter with her first garden when she was four years old. Once the marigolds and bush beans were planted, she tired of periodically asking, "What should I do, Papa?" (Besides pick beans and flowers, of course.) My own vegetable garden—about 2,000 square feet of beds and paths—demands less than five minutes of weeding per week to keep it essentially weed-free.

Cleanup Time

Both esthetics and practicality drive us to tidy up the garden. As cheery as marigolds, cosmos, and other annuals flowers are through the summer, they have to go when blackened by frost. The vegetable garden presents a steady progression of plants that have overstayed their welcome, from old lettuces gone to seed in late spring and bush beans that have petered out by midsummer to tomato vines blackened by frost come fall. Perennial flowers also need periodic tidying, even though they return year after year.

On the practical side, removing last season's plants is necessary to make room for next season's plants or seeds. Once midsummer arrives and the bush beans, no longer bearing well, are out of the way, a later crop—of, say, beets or carrots—can be planted. Clearing last year's dead marigold plants makes way for this year's plants.

Cleaning away old or spent plants also decreases problems that result from a number of pests that survive from one season to the next on their remains. Gray mold disease of peonies, which prevents the sumptuous flower buds from opening, overwinters on old, infected peony leaves and stems. Cut them off after they die back at the end of the season, cart them away, and voila! you have put distance between the fungal spores and the new leaves they are looking to infect. The European corn

A quick twist severs fine roots of small plants, which can then be removed while hardly disturbing the soil.

borer—an insect that bores into and
weakens stalks of corn and other
plants—similarly spends the winter in
old stalks.

In the Weedless Garden, clean
up cultivated annual plants when
they are no longer wanted by taking
away all of their tops and their
largest roots—with minimal disruption of the soil. Caring for the
soil from the top down promotes
an abundance of shallow roots
(which is good), but merely
tugging up plant stalks would
carry away all those roots and a

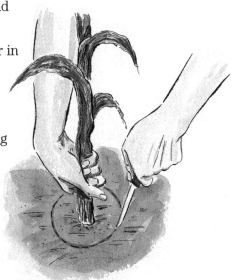

*Cut large roots of corn while twisting
and lifting the stalk out of the ground.*

goodly amount of attached soil. Roughly digging up old plants is as bad
for the soil and as encouraging to weeds as tilling.

To clean up large old annual flower or vegetable plants, take a
sturdy, sharp garden knife and pull up on a plant's stalk with one hand
while simultaneously working the knife up and down into the soil in a
circle right around the stalk. With old lettuces or cabbages, I dispense
with the knife and instead grab the head and give it a sharp twist
to sever smaller roots. If a plant has some large roots running deep
beneath its stalk—as some of corn's roots do—bend the stalk from side
to side, thrusting the knife into the ground opposite to where the stalk
is bent.

With small roots severed, most stalks lift right up out of the ground.
Small roots that remain in the ground rot too fast to provide a winter
home for pests, but they do enrich the soil and leave small channels for

water, air, and subsequent living roots. The ground can be replanted without delay, an impossibility when ground is cleared traditionally because you then have to wait for all the debris tilled into the soil to decompose.

Clean up perennial flowers by breaking or cutting off old stalks and leaves, then carting them away. No finesse is required.

All this is not to say that any vegetable or flower garden should go into winter looking bare. Not every stalk or leaf is harboring some insect or disease ready to pounce come spring. Leaving some old plants, such as the bristly heads of coneflower and teasel, as well as the leaves and seed heads of certain ornamental grasses, dresses up the otherwise barren landscape of cold winters.

Mulch

Nature abhors bare ground and so should you. Her response to naked earth is to clothe it, a job at which many weeds excel. What Weedless Gardening does is keep the ground covered with something else, which, among other things, will prevent weeds from getting a foothold. Mulch, the catch-all term for a host of different ground blankets, is the preferred alternative to leaving soil exposed to weeds.

Why do we and Mother Nature hate bare soil? Because the naked surface is too easily blown and washed away by wind and water. Rainfall pounding on it seals pores, making it much harder for water to penetrate. This further contributes to erosion, an effect that snowballs as moving water increases speed to carve out rivulets, then gullies. Bare soil is also beat upon by sunlight, creating a hot, dry root environment.

Keeping the ground surface covered does more than keep weeds at

Malicious Mulch

Concern is sometimes voiced that spreading a nitrogen-poor mulch such as wood chips or sawdust over the soil will starve plants. The microorganisms that decompose these materials do indeed need nitrogen, and they are able to garner it at the expense of plants. But when wood chips or sawdust is laid on top of the soil, decomposition occurs mostly at the interface of the soil and the mulch—at a very slow rate. So slowly, in fact, that a steady state usually exists where nitrogen is re-released back into the soil sufficiently fast for plants growing there. These materials will surely starve plants, temporarily, when their decomposition is sped up by being thoroughly mixed into the soil.

bay and protect it from the elements. On paths, a surface covering diffuses pressure from footsteps, wheelbarrow wheels, and tractor tires. Plants aren't growing in paths, but rainfall still must penetrate soil there and some roots of plants bordering paths find their way there. In planted beds, mulch has the additional benefit of helping enrich soil and feed plants.

Ground originally prepared for Weedless Gardening was covered with paper and topped by some other material. To maintain the garden's surface, use the same mulch as you did when starting it. (The paper, however, was put down to quell existing vegetation and should never be needed again.)

Except for stones, bricks, and other inorganic materials that might be used for paths and rarely if ever need replenishing, all other materials used to cover the ground will be organic and do need regular renewal. Possible materials could be the same straw, wood chips, pine needles, leaves, or sawdust that you used to initially cover beds and paths. (See the Mulch Guide on pages 24–25 for materials.)

With time, organic materials decompose; this is why they must be

Temporarily laid along edges of a vegetable bed, 2" × 4" lumber makes spreading compost in that bed quick and neat.

continually replenished to maintain about a 1-inch depth or more over the surface. Don't begrudge these materials for disappearing, though. As they do so, they enrich the ground with soil-building humus, release nutrients into the soil, and nourish beneficial soil microorganisms. By laying these materials on top of the ground rather than digging them in, their goodness gradually seeps in for long-lasting benefits.

How frequently mulch needs to be replenished depends on how quickly it decomposes, which, in turn, depends on the material and the climate. Hot, moist weather speeds decomposition along most rapidly. Generally, I mulch-dress my whole garden in fall because that's when certain materials, such as leaves, are available. This also gives me less to do during the flurry of spring gardening activities, and the materials have all winter to begin melding with the underlying layer of soil. Trees, shrubs, and informal flower beds generally get a blanket of autumn leaves or wood chips (and blueberries get sawdust, which they particularly like). The vegetable garden goes

Good Chips, Bad Chips

Each spring, stores become awash in wood chips and bark chips. Besides the usual supply available at nurseries and garden centers, clean white bags of chips are neatly stacked at the front of hardware stores, supermarkets, and even convenience stores.

Some gardeners believe that chips sold in bags are superior to those made from locally chipped trees. One fear is that termites will infest wood other than the cedar often used for bagged chips, but there's no need for concern. Termites feed on a variety of cellulose sources, including old roots, twigs, and other materials in and on the ground; a mulch of chips would contribute insignificantly to the existing smorgasbord.

There might also be worry about diseases from locally chipped dead trees infecting the plants where the chips are spread. Again, it's not a problem. Most fungi that attack living wood cannot survive on deadwood and would expire in the chips. Fungi are also somewhat choosy in just what they attack. Even if you spread chips from a diseased pine tree beneath your maple tree, the maple is not going to get sick unless the disease survives in dead chips and is capable of infecting maple as well as pine, and conditions are conducive to the spread of that disease. The odds of this are perhaps akin to being hit by lightning on a sunny day.

Another criticism of local chips as opposed to bagged cedar chips is that the local stuff decomposes faster. True, but some of the benefits of chips accrue only as they decompose. Local chips will need more frequent replacement, but they are relatively cheap and sometimes free.

To get a load of local wood chips, look in the Yellow Pages under "Tree Service," or beg some from a landscaping crew working nearby. Local arborists are usually happy to unload chips at your house in lieu of hauling them to a landfill.

into winter with a fresh dressing of wood chips on the paths and a slather of rich brown compost on each bed (except for those still carrying late crops). At minimum, the time to replenish any mulch—

whether it's wood chips, compost, or straw—is as soon as bare soil begins to peek through.

Cover Crops

Cover crops, plants grown specifically to improve the soil, present an exciting alternative not only to weeding, but also to hauling mulch and even fertilizing. Dense growth of cover crops can shade weeds and provide organic materials that you would otherwise have to gather up or purchase, then spread. Some cover crops, such as rye, oats, sorghum-sudangrass hybrids, and subterranean clover, have an "alleopathic" effect; that is, they combat weeds by releasing natural, weed-suppressing chemicals into the soil. Cover crops also help nourish your plants by pulling up nutrients from deep within the soil, by increasing the availability of nutrients locked up in soil minerals, and by clinging to nutrients that rainwater might otherwise wash beyond the reach of roots.

Cover crops can do even more: After these plants die, their rotting roots leave behind channels for new roots, water, and air, and enrich

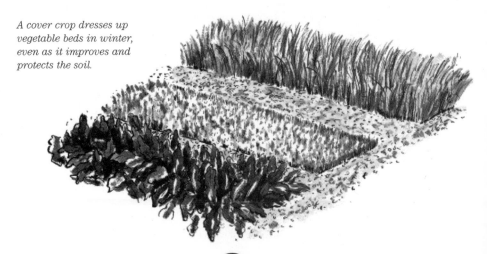

A cover crop dresses up vegetable beds in winter, even as it improves and protects the soil.

the soil with humus. Some cover crops can even act as "subsoilers," breaking up compacted layers within the soil. Some, like buckwheat, attract beneficial insects to decrease pest problems. And finally, the garden simply looks prettier in winter with the ground covered by a dense stand of plants than it does bare.

Where Can They Grow?

Enthusiasm for cover crops could come screeching to a halt with the question of where to put these wonderful plants when you already have a full garden. In a vegetable or annual flower garden, cover crops might grow when the ground would otherwise be bare, such as from late fall to early spring. Or a different part of a vegetable or flower garden might be set aside each year for a whole season's growth of a cover crop. In perennial borders or mixed borders of perennials and shrubs, cover crops can grow among plants for part of the season, then again during the cool months. The right cover crop might even look decorative among (other) ornamental plants. The show from crimson clover—its blossoms clustered tightly on upright stalks like crimson popsicles—is so spectacular that you'd hardly suspect it was improving the soil.

The Community of Cover Crops

There is no "best" cover-crop plant. Which one to grow depends on when you are going to plant, what your climate is like, and what, specifically, you want from the cover crop.

Most plants used for cover crops are either grasses or legumes. "Grasses" here means the whole grass family, from lawn grasses to grains such as rye, barley, and wheat. As cover crops, grasses are valued for their extensive roots (a total root length of 385 miles has been

CHARACTERISTICS OF SELECTED COVER CROPS

LEGUMES	TYPE	HARDINESS ZONE	HEAT TOLERANCE	SHADE TOLERANCE	DROUGHT TOLERANCE
Berseem clover	SA, WA	7	3	2	3
Cowpeas	SAL	NFT	4	3	2
Crimson clover	WA, SA	7	2	1	3
Field peas	WA	7	1	1	1
Hairy vetch	WA, CSA	4	1	2	2
Medics	SP, SA	4, 7	4	3	3
Red clover	SP, B	4	1	1	3
Subterranean clover	CSA	7	2	1	1
Sweet clover	B, SA	4	3	4	1
White clover	LP, WA	4	2	2	3
Woollypod vetch	CSA	7	3	3	2

NON-LEGUMES	TYPE	HARDINESS ZONE	HEAT TOLERANCE	SHADE TOLERANCE	DROUGHT TOLERANCE
Annual ryegrass	WA	6	1	1	3
Barley	WA	7	3	3	2
Buckwheat	SA	NFT	2	0	1
Oats	CSA	8	1	1	1
Rape	CSA	7	2	1	3
Rye	CSA	3	2	3	3
Sorghum-sudangrass	SA	NFT	4	4	2
Wheat	WA	4	2	2	2

K E Y

Type: B=biennial, CSA=cool-season annual, LP=long-lived perennial, SA=summer annual, SP=short-lived perennial, WA=winter annual
Hardiness zones: U.S.D.A. ratings; NFT=not frost-tolerant
Other ratings: 0=poor, 1=fair, 2=good, 3=very good, 4=excellent

Sow @ Oz./100 Sq. Ft.	Subsoiler	Alleopathic	Chokes Weeds	Ease of Mow-kill
2	1	1	3	1
5	2	0	4	4
2–3	1	1	2	3
4	1	1	3	4
2	2	2	3	4
2–3	2	1	3	3
3	3	2	2	1
3	0	3	4	0
1.5	4	1	2	3
1.5	1	2	3	2
2–3	3	2	4	4

Sow @ Oz./100 Sq. Ft.	Subsoiler	Alleopathic	Chokes Weeds	Ease of Mow-kill
1	2	2	4	4
3–5	2	3	3	4
3–4	0	3	4	4
4–6	0	3	4	1
1/8	4	3	3	4
3–6	1	4	4	4
2	4	4	4	3
3–4	2	1	3	3

measured beneath a single rye plant!). These roots plow through the soil to keep it loose, and upon dying, contribute to long-term fertility.

Legumes include familiar garden plants like peas and beans, as well as various types of clovers, vetches, and medics. Roots of leguminous cover crops harbor beneficial bacteria that extract nitrogen from the air and put it in a form usable by plants. Legume roots, however, are not as dense as those of grasses and they generally do not provide as much long-term soil improvement.

Planting grasses and legumes together can tap the benefits of each, and the right combinations can bring more specific benefits. A planting of sudangrass, alfalfa, or yellow mustard, for example, is good at breaking up compacted soil. Where the soil needs loosening in its lower depths, you might try a crop of sweet clover or some sorghum-sudangrass hybrid. Where fertility is low, a crop of buckwheat or sweet clover helps release nutrients such as phosphorus and potassium from soil minerals. Annual ryegrass, sorghum-sudangrass hybrids, rye, and subterranean clover are excellent soil builders for Eastern soils; subterranean clover, medics, and barley are especially good for this purpose in the West.

If weeds are threatening, smother them with a thick stand of annual ryegrass, rye, sorghum-sudangrass, buckwheat, barley, oats, cowpeas, subterranean clover, or woollypod vetch. Cut and allowed to lie on the surface of the ground, dead rye suppresses weeds first by smothering them and then by releasing natural, weed-suppressing chemicals into the soil for 30 to 60 days. In one study, rye effectively reduced pigweed by 95 percent, ragweed by 43 percent, and purslane by 100 percent. The effect is only on small seeds, so it's possible to plant large seeds such as corn, cucumber, or lupine right into the downed rye.

Note that the aforementioned yellow mustard and buckwheat are neither legumes nor grasses, but are useful cover crops nonetheless. (The mustard also decreases problems from soil-borne pests called nematodes.) And certain plants such as sudangrass, buckwheat, and cowpeas thrive only when grown in warm summer months. (See the Selected Cover Crops chart on pages 50–51 for characteristics and uses.)

All's Well That Ends Well

How do you deal with cover crops once they serve their purpose? Annual plants eventually die, flopping down on the ground, but not necessarily on schedule. For instance, rye (the grain) is a cover crop usually planted in early fall. It grows in cool weather, goes dormant in winter, then starts growing again at the first hint of spring. The plant matures by summer, ripening grain, then dies. If you use rye in a vegetable garden, the problem is that you won't want to wait until summer to plant vegetables.

The conventional way to kill a rye cover crop before its natural time is by tilling it into the soil as soon as possible in spring. But tilling would disrupt the soil, bring up weed seeds, burn humus, and bury the rye stalks and stems.

In Weedless Gardening we find other ways to kill cover crops, ways that need not disrupt the soil. Simplest of course is to grow something that dies by itself at the right moment. In my vegetable garden, I plant oats in any beds that become free of vegetables before the middle of September. Oats enjoy the cool weather, grow on into winter, and eventually are done in by temperatures dipping near 0°F. The plants then flop down on the ground dead, their leaves and stems still protecting the surface. Come spring it takes no more than my bare hands or a grass rake to "roll up" the dead leaves and stems (like a carpet) before planting. Woollypod vetch and barley are other cool-season plants that can be used similarly where winter lows drop near 0°F. Seeds of either of these plants might also be scattered within a perennial flower or shrub border (if not too shady) toward the end of the season to further enrich the soil and smother any late-season weeds trying to creep in.

With other annual cover crops, or where winter temperatures are not sufficiently low to kill cover crops, planting schedules in a flower or vegetable garden can be adjusted to accommodate the cover crop's natural death. Any sacrifice of space can be minimized by devoting only part of a garden to such a cover crop.

Winter-killed oats are easily "rolled up" to make way for spring planting.

Another way to bring a premature death to many kinds of cover crop plants is by mowing. (See the Selected Cover Crops chart on pages 50–51, for cover crops especially willing to succumb to mowing.) The timing for effective kill is critical, usually just before the plant is getting ready to flower. With some cover crops, two or three mowings would be most effective.

In a small garden, grass shears can be used for mow killing. A sickle, scythe, weed whacker, or power mower does the job in larger areas. Around woody plants or in areas slated for large seeds or transplants, the clipped stems and leaves might not interfere with planting. In this

Seed Sources for Cover Crops

• Fedco Seeds, P.O. Box 520, Waterville, ME 04903, 207-873-7333, www.fedcoseeds.com

• Harmony Farm Supply & Nursery, P.O. Box 460, Graton, CA 95444, 707-823-9125, www.harmonyfarm.com

• Johnny's Selected Seeds, 1 Foss Hill Road, R.R.1, Box 2580, Albion, ME 04910, 207-437-9294, www.johnnyseeds.com

• Peaceful Valley Farm Supply, P.O. Box 2209, Grass Valley, CA 95945, 530-272-4769, www.groworganic.com

• Seedway Inc., P.O. Box 250, Hall, NY 14463, 800-836-3710, www.seedway.com

• Welter Seed & Honey Co., 17724 Highway 136, Onslow, IA 52321, 800-728-8450

• Wolf River Valley Seeds, N2976 County M, White Lake, WI 54491, 715-882-3100, 800-359-2480

case, just leave them in place, letting the plants' dead tops protect the soil as their roots improved it. One advantage of leaving the mowings in place is that they'll release their nitrogen (which is present mostly in their above-ground portions) right back into the soil within a month or two in warm weather. Where mowings would interfere with planting, push them aside to leave just enough space for planting, or rake them off entirely.

Sprouting Innovations

The simplest way to deal with a cover crop is to plant it, then kill it at a later date. Innovative strategies for using cover crops more effectively and with less fuss are on the horizon. Consider the possibility of a cover crop permanently protecting and improving the soil, a living mulch. An obvious pitfall to this strategy is the living mulch acting like a weed and starving garden plants for food, water, or light. Sidestep this problem by choosing a cover crop plant that is not very competitive, or by periodically weakening it. Both white clover and perennial ryegrass have been used with varying degrees of success as living mulches between vegetable plants, with the growth of the cover crops weakened by periodic mowing.

An even more elegant possibility is a cover crop that plants itself to grow only when it would not interfere with cultivated plants. Subterranean clover and crimson clover are two such cover crops for regions with mild, moist winters. Planted in late summer, either of these clovers will sprout, then thrive in the cool, moist weather of fall and early winter. The plants go dormant in midwinter, reawaken when the weather warms, then set seed and die in spring. "Subterranean" highlights the subterranean clover's knack for sowing its own seeds right on or below the ground's surface. Hard-seeded varieties of either clover are slow to sprout, and wait until late summer or fall to initiate the cycle again.

Another unique use of cover crops is in the strawberry bed. Recent research has shown that after fruiting, June-bearing strawberry plants are very tolerant of shade. A cover crop—of oats, for example—sown right in the strawberry bed after the berries have been gathered can shade out weeds through the growing season, then eventually flop down dead to provide the mulch in which strawberry plants thrive.

As you have no doubt fathomed by now, there is no single recipe for best utilizing a cover crop in your own "back forty." All sorts of possibilities exist if you take the time to study specific cover crop plants and then experiment.

The question remains whether cover crops can totally replace wood chips, straw, compost, and other organic materials that would otherwise blanket the soil. Time will tell. For now, I integrate cover crops with imported materials (such as neighbors' leaves or manure from a horse farm), sprinkling oats or crimson clover in shrub borders, and having some vegetable beds go into winter with a sprinkling of soybean meal and a dense stand of oats growing up through a blanket of compost.

Containing Weeds

After adopting Weedless Gardening, you will have a new perspective on weeding. I now consider it to be a pleasant diversion, something I might do for a few moments in the course of a stroll through the garden. There's nothing inherently distasteful about weeding; after all, children don't consider it so until they have to do too much of it, or learn that no one else thinks it's fun.

But I cannot emphasize too strongly the need to keep an eye out for weeds on a regular basis. When I wander out to my garden to harvest, to sniff, to look at, or otherwise enjoy the plants, I often take a moment to pull a few weeds. Every couple of weeks, I'll do a regular patrol.

The reason to keep a vigilant eye out for weeds is not to keep them all out of the garden at all times, but to keep them from getting too big. Big weeds are a lot harder to remove than small ones, and when weeds get old enough, they start spreading underground or making seeds—over 100,000 seeds from a single plant of redroot pigweed! It is a sea of large weeds that drives some gardeners to flail at their ground with a large-bladed hoe better suited for mixing concrete than tending plants. A better way to deal with a sea of weeds

Weeds can enter a garden by air or by land.

grown out of hand through neglect is to start again with the paper and mulch.

Whence the Weeds?

Initial preparation of the weedless garden left sleeping weed seeds lying undisturbed within the soil, surface weeds smothered, and the ground iced with compost, wood chips, or some other weed-free material. So where now do the weeds come from?

Look first to your "weed-free" mulch. Such material is not necessarily 100 percent weed-free. A few weed seeds might get mixed into a bale of straw and a few seeds, such as tomato, tolerate heat to emerge viable from the innards of a hot compost pile.

Weed seeds also hitchhike. Dandelion seeds are perfectly engineered to parachute into a garden with the help of wind. Wild blackberries turn up in the garden after their seeds are dropped by passing birds. Mice, water, the bottom of your shoes, and insects all have the potential to transport weed seeds.

The edge of any planted area offers another opening for weed encroachment. Here weeds might crawl in stealthily, making their way via trailing stems, as does ground ivy (a.k.a. creeping Charlie) in parts of my garden. A weed might interlope even more surreptitiously, its roots or stems pushing underground some distance, before a furtive shoot pokes above ground. In my very first garden, the needle-sharp specialized stems of quackgrass traveled just beneath the surface of the ground to eventually enmesh it in a frightening lacy network. A truckload of seaweed cured that problem, but the smell was horrendous for a while.

Weed Patrol

Edges are a good place to start regular patrol. Weedwise, take care of the edges of planted areas, and the "middles" will (almost) care for themselves. Quackgrass still relentlessly pushes its sharp underground stems through the soil in an effort to gain entry at one end of my flower bed. If I turn it away there, I rarely see it within the bed. Floppy stems of ground ivy strain incessantly into one end of my vegetable garden like the horse that strains to eat the grass just outside its fenced pasture. Once again, I keep that edge in order and rarely find ground ivy among the vegetables. Mowing bordering land also keeps weed seeds at bay.

Within a garden that has not been neglected, weeds mostly appear either as a patch of many little ones or as a few big ones. These two situations need different approaches, even though the weeds will be done in with minimal disruption of the soil in either case.

Where weeds are few just pull them up individually, roots and all,

and put them into a bucket for eventual dumping on the compost pile. If pulling a weed threatens to take along enough soil to leave a crater, give the whole plant a sharp twist or use a sharp knife to slice off fine roots, leaving them behind as you pull out the stem and larger roots.

Deep-rooted weeds, such as dandelion and dock, probably will need coaxing before they'll even budge. Force a trowel (or for a really big weed, a long, narrow-bladed shovel) into the ground alongside the weed's taproot. Get a firm grip on the plant's crown with one hand, then pull as you gingerly lever the plant up with the

Lever deep-rooted weeds out of the soil with the help of a shovel or trowel.

trowel or shovel. Don't push the handle so far that you lift soil out of a newly created hole. You should be lifting the soil only slightly, keeping soil layers intact and hardly disrupting them. Once the large roots have torn free from the smaller ones, the bulk of the root will slide out as the soil drops back in place.

This may seem like a lot of time to spend with individual weeds, but there are not many of them and only a few will need two-handed coaxing. Best of all, a particular weed will never come back to haunt you once pulled roots and all. Rototill a big, fat dandelion or just chop its leaves off with a hoe, and you can expect repeat performances.

Where a colony of small weed plants is invading an area, pulling individual members is too tedious—and unnecessary. The way to do in these interlopers is to cut them off just beneath the soil surface, perhaps a quarter of an inch deep. Leave the severed "plantlets" in place; they're too small to revive and will wither within a short while.

Hoes that are perfect for this job include the colinear hoe, the hula hoe, and the winged weeder (my favorite). These tools all have sharp blades that naturally lie parallel to the ground when in use. An old steak knife with its blade bent at a right angle also does this job effectively. It is the tool—conveniently hung alongside the gate to my vegetable garden—I use for occasional small patches of weeds.

Colinear hoe

Weeds rarely appear in paths, and those that do are easily pulled out. With loose materials such as gravel or wood chips, periodic raking is enough to discombobulate most weed seedlings trying to gain a foothold—especially if it's done regularly. Relatively nontoxic herbicides based on soap or vinegar are also available to kill weeds. Paths of brick, stone, gravel, or other nonorganic materials call for their own weeding techniques. Heat is effective, either with a carefully directed blowtorch (large ones are made for this purpose) or with boiling water or steam. As with any other method of weeding, all these techniques are most effectively applied to small weeds. Except for herbicide applications, use these techniques regularly—before you even see weeds.

The situation may sometimes arise where a major weeding of some part of a garden is needed. Perhaps a portion of the garden has become weedy through nothing more than neglect; or a load of compost was not really weed-free. Then there was the time when my five-year-old daughter plucked dandelions from the

Hula hoe

lawn to playfully blow their seeds about. How could I quell such exuberance (the effects of which were only appreciated—by me—months, then years, later)? My advice, when more than a little weeding is called for, is to just do the job that needs to be done, slowly and thoroughly. If weeds get frighteningly out of hand, go back to laying down paper and covering it (see page 23).

Winged weeder.

The number of words devoted here to weeding belies the amount of time actually needed to do it. The first few years after I started gardening from the top down, I actually worried a little about how few weeds I found. I thought perhaps there was something wrong with the soil. I've since calmed down enough to actually enjoy the few minutes per week I now spend weeding.

CHAPTER FOUR

Coaxing Plants Further Along

For many plants, just about any mulch will suffice in keeping growth chugging along year after year; others need a bit more coaxing. Fertilizer, compost, and/or irrigation can lend a hand, when needed, in Weedless Gardening. As before, we will continue to follow Mother Nature's lead and let millions of years of evolution take charge.

How do you know when plants will need some extra coaxing? First, it depends on what plants you're growing. A 50-year-old maple tree with a well-established root system needs less help than a row of lettuce plants that are in and out of the garden in less than three months and during that time get their outer leaves picked off. Other considerations are soil, climate, and to a lesser extent, the kinds of mulches you use. Soils vary in their natural fertility and moisture-holding capabilities; poor or dry soils may need to be beefed up. The warmer the climate, the quicker plants grow and the faster mulches and nutrients disappear. An integral part of Weedless Gardening is keeping an eye on your plants—they often tell you what they need.

Feeding

Look at fertilizers on display at any garden center, and the first thing you see are numbers. Lots of them: 5-10-5, 10-10-10, 5-5-5, 30-10-10. You might also notice specific fertilizers for roses, tomatoes, bulbs—as if each kind of plant needs its own special pabulum. Look more closely and you might even find fertilizers for "spring feeding" or for "summer feeding." It's a wonder such plants can live together in a single garden.

Ignore all the fertilizer hype. It's confusing and induces you to purchase more fertilizer than you need.

The Main Course

It would be wonderful if we never had to feed our plants. However, some nutrients are naturally lost when washed away by rainfall, a soil can be naturally deficient in some nutrient, and you do carry nutrients off-site when harvesting vegetables, fruits, and flowers. On the other hand, soils naturally enrich themselves to some extent, releasing nutrients locked up in minerals and even converting atmospheric nitrogen to plant food.

The kinship of Weedless Gardening methods with those of Mother Nature allows you, in many situations, to dispense with fertilization per se—in the sense of having to spread some powdered, concentrated, bagged material. Organic mulch that constantly blankets the ground is just as constantly decomposing. The resulting witches' brew of compounds in the soil becomes food for plants, releases plant foods previously locked up in the rocky matrix of the soil, and facilitates plant uptake of some foods already dissolved in the soil water. Mulch alone usually provides enough food for the relatively minimal needs of wildflowers and established trees and shrubs.

Vegetables, flowers planted in a formal bed, and young trees, shrubs, and vines are generally hungrier plants. We demand a bit more oomph from a stalk of celery—it has to be extra succulent. Formal flowers are called on to provide an intense, nonstop show of blossoms. And young woody plants must quickly fill their allotted space. An organic mulch might still directly and indirectly supply all that's needed by these plants in a naturally rich soil, depending on how intensely they're grown. If the organic mulch is compost, which is relatively rich in food, so much the better.

If fertilizer is needed for naturally poor soil or for intensively planted vegetables, there's no need to go back to the fertilizer display and wade through numbers, fertilizer types, and timing. More often than not, when Weedless Gardening from the top down, the only nutrient that *might* need to be deliberately added in the form of a concentrated, powdered, bagged material is nitrogen. Nitrogen is the first of three numbers prominently displayed on fertilizer packaging (the other two numbers represent phosphate and potash, two forms of phosphorus and potassium).

The Universal Pabulum

Among the best nitrogen sources—the one that I use almost exclusively—is soybean meal. It is a universal, "one size fits all" pabulum appropriate for all plants—as good for roses as it is for tomatoes, and equally effective for plants that need acid soils and those that need alkaline soils. Soybean meal is ground up,

Sprinkle soybean meal, if needed, right on top of planting beds.

de-fatted soybeans whose protein is slowly broken down by soil microorganisms to become nitrogen that plants can use. It is "organic," cheap, and available at feed stores. As a general recommendation, use 3 pounds of soybean meal per 100 square feet of planted area, and spread it once a year before laying down any kind of mulch. What could be simpler?

Concentrated Organic Sources for Major Nutrients

NITROGEN: soybean meal, cotton-seed meal, alfalfa meal, blood meal, leather dust, poultry manure, fish emulsion, guano, hair, hoof and horn dust

PHOSPHORUS: colloidal phosphate, rock phosphate, guano, bonemeal

POTASSIUM: wood ash, granite dust, greensand (glauconite), Sul-Po-Mag (langbeinite)

Cottonseed meal is another nitrogen fertilizer, equivalent to soybean meal but more expensive. You could also use a ubiquitous 5-10-10 or 10-10-10 fertilizer, the three numbers indicating the percentages of nitrogen, phosphorus, and potassium, respectively. For now, we're interest in supplying nitrogen, so adjust the rate of any fertilizer according to how much nitrogen it contains. Generally, our aim is to apply 2/10 pound of actual nitrogen per 100 square feet, whether the nitrogen comes from 2 pounds of 10-10-10 (2 pounds fertilizer × 10%N = 0.2 pound nitrogen), 4 pounds of 5-10-10 (4 pounds fertilizer × 5%N = 0.2 pound nitrogen), or 3 pounds of soybean or cottonseed meal (3 pounds fertilizer × 7%N = 0.2 pound nitrogen).

Anything Else on the Menu?

Most of your plants probably won't need any bagged, conventional fertilizer other than some soybean meal, if that, but still keep a vigilant eye on them for signs of starvation. Hungry plants won't squeal like

Organic vs. Synthetic Fertilizers

"**O**rganic" fertilizers are natural materials that supply plant nutrients in their raw state or after slight processing. Manures, ground-up rocks, and composted vegetable wastes are examples of organic fertilizers. These fertilizers generally provide plants with a long, slow feed of a nutrient smorgasbord, and their manufacture puts minimum demand on the planet's natural resources.

In contrast, chemical fertilizers are relatively pure compounds, usually synthesized in factories. They are concentrated sources of nutrients that, in most cases, are quickly available to plants but can also quickly wash out of the soil or burn plant roots.

Despite the potential benefits of organic fertilizers, many gardeners make the mistake of using them in the same way as synthetic ones. For instance, a gardening "expert" on the radio was touting the benefits of guano, or bat droppings. He was right about guano's being rich in nutrients—almost 20 percent nitrogen in a form that can be taken up quickly by plants. And guano is definitely natural—it's scooped out of caves where bats hang out. The problem is that guano doesn't differ much in its effects on plants and soil from 20-10-10 or any other quick-acting synthetic fertilizer. The same could be said for blood meal, poultry manure, and other concentrated, quick-acting organic fertilizers.

What is missing from all synthetic fertilizers and from concentrated organic fertilizers is bulk, which comes from organic materials rich in carbon. Types of raw bulk are straw, autumn leaves, sawdust, hay, and manures. (Most of the bulk associated with manures comes from the sawdust, straw, or other material used for animal bedding.) Bulky materials such as compost, peat moss, and old manure become stabilized through decomposition. The benefits of bulk include getting soils to hold more air and water, making plant foodstuffs already in the soil more available, and helping plants fight off certain diseases.

The lesson is, don't necessarily seek out the most concentrated or "richest" organic fertilizer. And if you do use a concentrated fertilizer, add plenty of bulky organic materials along with it.

ANALYSIS OF SOME CONCENTRATED ORGANIC FERTILIZERS

Material	% Nitrogen	% Phosphorus	% Potassium	Plant Availability
Alfalfa meal	3	1	2	Moderately fast
Bat guano	8–19	4–31	2	Fast
Bird guano	8–13	8–15	2	Fast
Blood meal	15	1	1	Fast
Bone meal	3–6	20	0	Slow; steamed faster than raw
Colloidal phosphate	0	20	0	Part of phosphorus available fast
Compost	1–3	0.5–1	1–3	Slow
Fish emulsion	4–5	2–4	1–2	Fast
Fish meal	9	7	0	Fast
Granite dust	0	0	5	Slow, long-lasting
Greensand	0	1	5–7	Slow, long-lasting
Leather meal	6–12	0	0	Part of nitrogen available fast
Manure, cow	0.25	0.15	0.25	Moderately fast
Manure, horse	0.3	0.15	0.5	Moderately fast
Manure, poultry	2–6	2–4	1–3	Fast
Peat	1–3	0.25–0.5	0.5–1	Very slow
Rock phosphate	0	33	0	Slow
Seaweed	1–2	0–1	5–13	Fast
Seed meal (soy, cottonseed)	7	2	2	Medium to fast
Sewage sludge	2–6	3–7	0–1	Slow to moderately slow
Wood ashes	0	1–2	3–7	Fast
Worm castings	1	0	0	Slow

starving pigs, but they can tell you when they're hungry, and for what (see the box at right). Low-level hunger might result in stunted growth that can go unrecognized unless it's dramatic. More severe deficiencies result in misshapen or off-color leaves, fruits, or stems. Generally such problems should not arise in Weedless Gardening, where the constant stream of organic materials provides a smorgasbord of plant nutrients. Should symptoms present themselves, however, don't be too quick to lay the blame on your soil's lack of a particular nutrient. Off-color or misshapen leaves could also be traced to aphids, frost, virus diseases, or hail, among other things.

If lime or sulfur was needed initially, regular additions of either are likely to be needed to keep the soil acidity in a range to suit particular plants. A simple soil test provides this information. Sprinkle any needed lime or sulfur on top of the ground every year if needed, so it can work its way gradually down to the root zone.

Abundant organic matter goes a long way toward averting problems with maintaining correct soil acidity, just as it keeps plants well nour-

Nutrient Deficiency Symptoms

NITROGEN: stunted plants, yellowing leaves beginning with oldest ones, and early shedding of leaves

PHOSPHORUS: stunted plants, purplish leaf coloration of seedling leaves

POTASSIUM: tips and edges of leaves turn yellow and finally die, beginning with oldest leaves

CALCIUM: malformation or stunting of growing tips or youngest leaves, blackened ends of tomato or pepper fruits

MAGNESIUM: discoloration of areas between veins of young leaves, any shade from red to purple to yellow depending on the plant

SULFUR: stunted plants and yellowing of youngest leaves

IRON: areas between veins on youngest leaves turn yellow, with veins remaining green

ished. These materials buffer acidity, allowing for more slack in what plants feel is "just right." So keep chanting the mantra "organic matter."

Compost

Compost is the crumbly, sweet-smelling material left after organic materials—things that are or were once living—have decayed. Compost is not one thing, but a potpourri of natural compounds that has positive physical, biological, and nutritional effects on plants and soils.

How hungry your garden is for compost depends on what plants you grow, how closely you plant them, and how intently you coax them along. Almost all plants, from lettuce and larkspur to lilac or linden, enjoy a topdressing of compost over the ground—even if they don't really demand it. Like any good mulch, a blanket of compost snuffs out small, newly sprouted weeds attempting to establish a foothold. Also like any good mulch, that compost layer keeps the soil cool and moist for plant roots, and loose so water seeps in rather than seals the surface and skitters across it.

Compost really stands out from other mulches in the way it nourishes plants. It is relatively rich and well balanced in plant foods, both in concentration and in the range of nutrients offered. In general, an annual 1-inch-thick dressing supplies all the food any plant needs.

Purchasing Compost

For gardeners lacking the time, resources, or inclination to make enough of their own compost, a cottage industry has sprouted up throughout much of the country that recycles "waste" into compost. Generally, the material is very reasonably priced and usually can be delivered right to your doorstep—or wherever else you want it dumped. A bit of sleuthing before you buy, however, ensures that the compost you get is high-quality stuff.

I'm not talking about the bagged compost that has traditionally been available at garden centers; usually, it just doesn't pay to buy compost by the bag for the quantities you'll need. Also, packaged compost is dead. All those good microorganisms that thwart disease, gobble up foodstuffs to release plant foods, and make the soil nice and crumbly have been killed by sterilization.

Start your search for bulk compost in newspaper ads and the Yellow Pages. "Compost" is an obvious starting point, but depending on your telephone directory, you may draw a blank or a reference to "Topsoil," "Fertilizers," "Mulch," "Manure," or "Mushrooms." Anyone selling these materials may also be selling compost. Make sure that what's being sold *is* compost, not just an old pile of wood chips or manure sold under the nebulous term "black dirt." Some purveyors of compost even combine it with soil and then sell it as a "topsoil," so make sure you're getting pure compost that's not mixed with various other materials.

One-third of a cubic yard of compost is needed to cover 100 square feet, 1 inch deep.

Once you find someone who sells bona fide compost, a few pointed questions can help you determine the quality of the product. No matter what goes into making different composts, the finished products are all surprisingly similar in nutrient values for major plant foods. Nonetheless, ask what went into the compost; with all other things equal, a greater variety of raw materials will result in a better variety of nutrients in the end product. Especially in the vegetable garden, you'll want to avoid using compost that contains industrial wastes because of possible contamination of food by toxins such as heavy metals. In dry regions, composts made from feedlot manures might be excessively high in salts, which can cause burning of roots. Also ask about the acidity, or pH, of the finished product. The ideal compost for most garden plants is slightly acidic, with a pH between 6 and 7.

Many gardeners are bothered by rocks in their soil, so yet another question to ask is how rocky or stony the compost is. Besides the bother of the rocks, you don't want to be paying for them rather than compost.

To keep the Weedless Garden weedless, it is particularly important that viable weed seeds be few or absent from compost. You don't want the layer of rich brown compost that you spread on your soil to be transformed, with a little rain and sun, into a carpet of weeds. After all, part of the

Purchased in bulk, compost can be both high-quality and inexpensive.

reason you use compost is to smother the weeds below.

Time, temperature, and pile-turning all have a bearing on the number of viable weed seeds in finished compost. A carefully built compost pile easily reaches high enough temperatures to kill most weed seeds. Turning the pile gets it cooking again and eliminates any weed seeds that survived the first cooking. Even when weed-free initially, composts that sit around too long (especially if uncovered) will pick up weed seeds carried in by wind and animals.

> The weight of finished compost is from 900 to 1,500 pounds per cubic yard, depending on the moisture content.

Finally, get a sample of any compost before you get a truckload, if possible. The material should no longer contain obvious bits of raw materials, but should be brown and crumbly with the pleasant, earthy aroma of a forest floor.

Making Compost

Making compost can be as satisfying as making bread. A failed loaf of bread, however, is an inedible brick. Not so with compost. Given enough time, you get compost no matter what you do. The goal in building a compost pile is to produce a rich, dark, crumbly material containing few viable weeds in a reasonable amount of time and without offending anyone's eyes or nose. The way to do this is by providing the right conditions and foodstuffs for the microorganisms that create compost.

• **LOCATION, LOCATION:** Location is not quite as important in composting as it is in real estate, but it is the first thing to consider. Ideally, site a compost pile where you can conveniently bring materials to it and just as conveniently remove the finished compost near where you're going to spread it. This might mean putting the pile within footsteps of your kitchen door so you can conveniently dump food scraps, or where you can unload materials (such as manure or leaves) you haul in by car or truck. And you will have to haul in outside materials to make enough compost to meet the needs of any but the smallest vegetable or formal flower garden, unless you have a hayfield or keep livestock (in which case you either haul in or grow their bedding). Alternately, you might want the pile close to your garden, where you spread the finished compost.

For those who actually do the work of composting—bacteria, fungi, and earthworms—the ideal place for the pile is shaded in summer to prevent drying. Other times of year, these organisms appreciate sunlight for extra warmth. Trees with aggressive roots, such as silver maple and willow, are a no-no near a compost pile unless you promise to use the compost before tree roots make inroads into the finished material.

• **MY COMPOST FOR A BIN:** A compost pile is not a garbage pile, and one way to clearly differentiate the two is with an enclosure—a compost bin. A bin can fend off raccoons, stray dogs, and any other animals wanting to scavenge fresh ingredients. A bin also retains generated heat—especially important in autumn as outdoor temperatures cool—and can maintain moisture at a level that keeps microorganisms happily going about their work. This heat also helps kill insect and disease pests in old plant debris.

Possible materials for building compost bins are cinder blocks or stones, hay or straw bales stacked like bricks, and wood. When bales used to construct a bin rot, they can be added

A wire fence compost bin.

to the compost pile. A bin enclosed by a picket fence could match the picket fence around your garden or home. Slabwood, often free for the hauling from a sawmill, makes a bin that has the look of a rustic log cabin. Bins should be three-sided for easy access, or even better, with a fourth side as a door.

A three-sided compost bin made from cinder blocks.

My homemade "state of the art" compost bin is constructed from 1" × 12" hemlock boards, each 5 feet long, purchased rough-sawn from a sawmill. With two tabs cut out at each end, and a notch formed with a foot-long 1" × 2" crosspiece, these boards stack tier upon tier like Lincoln Logs. The structure is built up as I add raw materials for composting, then taken down, board by board, as I remove finished compost. By facing a different side inward each time I use a board, they have remained serviceable even after 10 years.

Wooden compost bins with removable fourth sides and a cover.

A bin is a minimum requirement for good compost. Become a compost maven, and you'll likely set up two or more bins. This system allows ingredients in one bin to age and mellow while materials are added to a second bin.

My homemade bin "grows" as materials are added.

Cold-Weather Compost

No matter how neatly a compost pile is kept in winter, not much happens in cold weather. Mounds of old salad, cooked broccoli, and moldy bread just sit. There won't be odors in winter, but it's not a pretty sight.

You can actively compost kitchen scraps in winter by doing it indoors. One way is with red worms, the kind that live in manure heaps and compost piles and are sold as fishing bait. Put the worms in a bin with a loose-fitting lid along with some shredded newspaper and a smidgen of soil. Then feed them kitchen waste as fast as they can eat it.

You can also compost indoors without worms. All you need are three buckets (5-gallon should suffice) with loose-fitting lids. Fill one with a mixture of equal parts dry sawdust (or peat moss) and dry soil, with a little limestone added.

To begin composting, put an inch of dry straw, leaves, or shredded newspaper into the bottom of one of the empty buckets. Dump your kitchen scraps into the bucket as they become available, each time sprinkling on some of the sawdust-soil mixture to absorb odors and excess moisture. If you have a lot of scraps at once, dump in a little at a time, covering each layer with the sawdust-soil mixture. Chop up large pieces and let water drain from anything that is very wet before you toss it into the bucket.

• **FILL 'ER UP:** When it comes to assembling raw materials for composting, it helps to look on your compost pile as an animal that needs air, water, and food. Provide air by making sure the pile is fluffy. Balance out materials like grass clippings or maple leaves, which mat down and become dense, with loose materials like corn, sunflower stalks, or

Layering materials into a compost bin helps you monitor how much of each you are adding.

When your bucket is full, set it aside somewhere warm and start filling the other empty bucket. By the time the second bucket is full, the contents of the first one will be well on the way to becoming compost, no longer looking like garbage and no longer attractive to scavengers. Dump the contents of the first bucket outside on your compost pile, and start filling that bucket again while the second one sits.

Left, bucket being filled with kitchen scraps. Center, soil-sawdust mix to cover each layer of scraps. Right, scraps composting in a filled bucket, to be emptied when first bucket is filled.

Keep the bucket you are filling plus the one with the sawdust-soil mixture right in the kitchen. Warmth hastens decomposition, and the whole setup is odor- and fly-free and at least as convenient as a garbage pail.

straw. Do not pile any materials higher than 5 feet or their own weight will compress air out of the bottom layers.

Rain can take care of watering your compost, but it takes a lot of rainfall to trickle down through 3 or more feet of spongy stems and leaves. I water my compost "animal" as I feed it, never adding more water than necessary to make the ingredients glisten. Once a compost bin is full, I give it one last watering, then cover the top with plastic to seal in the water that I have applied and to prevent rainfall from driving out air and making the ingredients soggy.

A MENU OF CARBON AND NITROGEN FOODS

Finished compost has a carbon (C) to nitrogen (N) ratio of about 20:1. Decomposition of materials with a ratio higher than this (that is, with excess carbon) is slow because microorganisms use what nitrogen they have to bring the ratio down by burning up excess carbon. Materials with ratios of less than 20 generally decompose quickly but lose their excess nitrogen as gas while they bring the carbon-nitrogen ratio up to 20. Combining high-carbon and high-nitrogen materials gives microorganisms both foods, conserving nitrogen and incorporating carbon into humus.

But things in Nature are not so straightforward, of course. The second column, Speed of N Availability, factors in the chemical makeup of these materials, which also influences how fast they can be gobbled up by microorganisms. And all other things being equal, larger particles make a quicker meal than do smaller ones.

MATERIAL	C:N RATIO	SPEED OF N AVAILABILITY
Alfalfa	21:1	Medium
Apple pomace	13:1	Medium fast
Blood, dried	4:1	Fast
Bonemeal	4:1	Slow
Cabbage	12:1	Medium
Cardboard	500:1	Slow
Carrot, whole	27:1	Medium
Chicken manure	36:1	Fast
Cocoa meal	15:1	Slow
Coffee grounds	20:1	Medium fast
Corn stalks	70:1	Slow
Cottonseed meal	5:1	Medium fast
Fish scraps, dried	4:1	Fast
Grass clippings	15:1	Fast
Guano	1:1	Fast

Material	C:N Ratio	Speed of N Availability
Hoof meal	3:1	Fast
Horse manure	33:1	Medium fast
Leaves	54:1	Slow
Milorganite	6:1	Medium fast
Newsprint	600:1	Slow
Oat straw	60:1	Slow
Peanut hull meal	54:1	Slow
Pig manure	14:1	Medium
Sawdust	500:1	Slow
Seaweed	19:1	Fast
Sewage sludge	14:1	Slow
Soybean meal	5:1	Medium fast
Urine	1:1	Fast
Wheat straw	197:1	Slow

Feed your compost almost anything that was once or is living. A wide variety of organic materials, from supermarket wastes to seaweed, are available free for the hauling. The only organic materials to exclude are fatty materials because they make your compost sluggish, and kitty litter because it can carry pathogens. Meat will compost, but it can be too attractive to neighborhood dogs and wilder creatures unless the bin is truly animal-proof. There is no need to add commercially available "compost activators." These products contain composting microorganisms that are so ubiquitous that adding them to a compost pile is like hauling coals to Newcastle.

Compost Concerns

As the bumper sticker on my truck reads, COMPOST HAPPENS, which is true—but not always as smoothly or quickly as intended.

Sluggishness or lack of heat in a compost pile is usually the result of insufficient nitrogen, too little or too much water, or too little air. The cure is to turn the pile, adding more nitrogen as you do so if it seems to have an overabundance of carbon foods, or more water if it seems too dry. Turning will also aerate a pile that was gasping for air because of too much water or too dense packing of raw materials. Even with a good balance of food, water, and air, a compost pile built up slowly or in cold weather will generate little heat.

Another potential composting problem is a malodorous pile or one that attracts flies. The cause here could be too little air or too much water; again, both problems are solved by turning the pile. Excess nitrogen also could be a cause. If so, turn the pile while incorporating some carbon-rich food such as wood chips or straw, or just wait for excess nitrogen to escape as gas.

In fact, you could wait out any compost problem because any pile of organic materials will eventually turn to compost. COMPOST HAPPENS.

Some gardening "experts" advise keeping insect or disease-ridden plants out of a compost pile to prevent the pests or pathogens from spreading. Balderdash! You'd have to exclude almost all plants if you examined them closely enough. Throwing any and all plants into my compost piles for decades has not caused pest problems in my garden.

In a compost pile, what spells death to insects, diseases, and weeds is some combination of heat and time. Pile up compostable materials in a big batch—with attention to the mix of ingredients, air, and moisture—and intense heat soon follows. The dial on my long-probed compost thermometer has spun as high as 160°F, which

Composting Bins and Things

Following are some sources for composting bins and related materials.

• Beaver River Associates, Josh Nelson, P.O. Box 94, West Kingston, RI 02892, 401-782-8747

• ComposTumbler, 160 Koser Road, Lititz, PA 17543, 800-880-2345, www.compostumbler.com

• Flowerfield Enterprises, 10332 Shaver Road, Kalamazoo, MI 49024, 616-327-0108, www.wormwoman.com

• Gardener's Supply Co., 128 Intervale Road, Burlington, VT 05401, 888-833-1412, www.gardeners.com

• Kinsman Company, P.O. Box 428, Pipersville, PA 18947, 800-733-4146, www.kinsmangarden.com

• Mellinger's, Inc., 2310 West South Range Road, North Lima, OH 44452, 800-321-7444, www.mellingers.com

• Recycled Plastics Marketing, 2829 152nd Ave. NE, Redmond, WA 98052, 425-867-3200, 800-867-3201, www.rrpm.com

is hot enough to do in virtually all pests in short order.

A casually made pile, or one that has been built gradually over a few weeks (especially in autumn as the weather is turning cold), will generate little heat. But let any pile of living or once-living material sit long enough, and the little heat generated will kill pests. A week at 100°F could have the same killing effect on a pest as an hour at 140°F. Eventually, resident pests will expire or be gobbled up by other microorganisms.

Two foods to keep in mind when feeding your compost are carbon and nitrogen. Carbon is abundant in old plant materials such as straw, leaves, sawdust, and paper—note that these are all dry and brown.

COMPOST WORKSHEET

If you become dedicated to making compost, and lots of it, it helps to sit down and start listing "waste materials." Here's a list of some things that have gone into my compost piles over the years, along with space for you to add things to put into your compost piles. There's also a place to keep a record of sources for compost, in case you buy it rather than make it yourself, or buy it to supplement your homemade concoction.

MY GARDEN	YOUR GARDEN
Hay from adjoining field	
Manure from horse farm	
Autumn leaves put out by neighbors	
Soybean meal	
Vegetable trimmings from kitchen	
Spent garden plants	
Grass clippings	
Wood chips	
Bedding & manure from chicken house	
Weeds mowed along roadsides	
Old bread & eggshells from bakery	
Old cotton sweater	
Weeds!	
SOURCES FOR BUYING COMPOST	**SOURCES FOR BUYING COMPOST**
Wedding Bell Farm, 895-2581	
Croswell Enterprises, 331-4232	
Bruderhof Communities, 658-8351	

Nitrogen is abundant in young, succulent plant materials—green stuff such as lettuce and cabbage leaves, vegetable parings, and grass clippings—as well as in manures. Nitrogen fertilizers are concentrated sources of this element, and are sometimes an ingredient (at inflated prices) of commercially available "compost activators." When my compost needs a concentrated source of nitrogen, I sprinkle on the same soybean meal that I occasionally use as fertilizer.

The ideal in feeding your compost is a balanced diet of both nitrogen-rich and carbon-rich foods. (In theory, 1 part nitrogen to 20 parts carbon is ideal.) If you are building up a pile gradually, keep handy a bale of hay, some straw, or a pile of wood chips to provide a carbon-rich food to periodically cover up layers of nitrogen-rich vegetable scraps. If you have a quantity of materials available all at once, build the pile with alternating layers of carbon and nitrogen foods. Layering materials lets you more objectively assess how much of each raw material you are adding to the pile.

How much nitrogen or carbon foodstuff is needed depends on the amount of nitrogen or carbon in the foodstuff, but don't fret over providing exactly balanced nutrition for your compost, grinding the raw materials, or turning the pile over. Let observation and experience be your guides. A long-probed compost thermometer and your nose are handy devices for keeping tabs on what's going on in a compost pile (see the box Compost Concerns on page 80).

Compost is never finished, but it does eventually become a somewhat stabilized material when ready to use. At that point, heat is no longer generated and most raw materials have been transmuted into a dark brown, crumbly fudge with a pleasant, woodsy aroma.

Drip Irrigation

Drip...drip...drip. We have now entered plant heaven, a place where plants are never wanting for water. We could be in a tropical rain forest, with water swept from fog dripping off the tips of tree leaves. Or we could be in a Weedless Garden, with water drip . . . drip . . . dripping to plant roots via a drip irrigation (sometimes called trickle irrigation) system. Drip irrigation uses inexpensive plastic pipe and specially designed water emitters to pinpoint water right where it's needed for the plant roots. As roots slowly draw in water to replenish that lost from leaves, emitters slowly replenish water into the soil.

Drip irrigation, or any sort of irrigation, is not an absolute necessity for growing plants in every part of the world. You might have to water transplants and seeds to get them going, and trees and shrubs for the first year or two, but beyond that, most plants more or less fend for themselves in most years, except in arid climates.

And there's the rub: "more or less fend for themselves in most years." Surviving is not the same as thriving. Rain rarely falls as soon as a plant needs water, so even in a wet summer, plants usually grow better with timely watering. And a freak dry season can have plants crying for water just to stay alive. The benefits of watering will depend on numerous factors: whether the plants are annuals, which must start from scratch, setting down roots for the year; how well adapted the

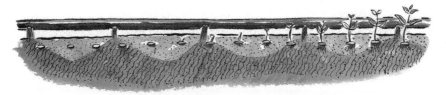

*Brief hand watering may be needed until
roots reach the zone of soil wetted by drip irrigation.*

plants are to the climate; how well the climate behaves; and how good a performance you want from your plants. With few exceptions, if you are going to water, drip irrigation is the way to go.

Benefits

Drip irrigation integrates seamlessly with other components of Weedless Gardening. There's no threat of rototillers, digging forks, or other tillage tools damaging the water lines because we're not tilling. And by pinpointing water right to plants, none is wasted or promoting weed growth in the ground between widely spaced plants or in paths. A sprinkler, on the other hand, democratically spreads water everywhere.

Drip irrigation almost completely does away with the need to trudge water to and around the garden. The only time this is necessary is to jump-start seeds or small transplants in dry soil, until their roots grow out. No need to move sprinklers around or even turn the water on and off. Drip irrigation is easily and inexpensively automated. And because water only has to slowly drip out of the emitters, the whole setup works with low water pressure and puts little demand on home wells.

What is the effect of all this dripping on plants? Let's contrast the effects of drip irrigation with those of sprinkler irrigation or furrow irrigation (whereby water is periodically channeled over the ground to inundate it). "Water deeply and infrequently to promote deep rooting" is the chant of gardeners who apply water with sprinklers or in furrows. At each watering, all the soil pores are initially filled. Only when gravity has drained water from larger pores can roots breathe again and utilize water still held in smaller, capillary pores. The water initially drained away is largely wasted, and the whole cycle is repeated on a regular, usually weekly schedule.

"Water shallowly and frequently" is the chant of drip-irrigation

gardeners. This way, plants are offered water at a rate more in synch with their ability to use it. Periodic inundation is avoided and wasteful. Roots have constant access to both water and air, and grow in the surface layers of soil—where biological activity, nutrients, and air are greatest.

In contrast to sprinkling, water from a drip system does not have to shoot through the air to get to plants, so evaporation before water gets into the soil is minimized (another contribution to the 60 percent water savings credited to drip irrigation). Another important benefit is that plants with dry leaves are much less subject to fungal diseases.

Soil pores, at left in each drawing, always hold water plus air with drip irrigation, shown below, in contrast to a feast-or-famine situation with a sprinkler, shown above.

Nuts and Bolts

Let's look at the components of a typical drip irrigation system, starting where the water exits near the plants and then wending our way back to the hose spigot.

The gizmos through which water finally exits are called emitters. More than just leaky pieces of plastic, the best of them have ingeniously designed orifices that are not prone to clogging and maintain a fairly constant drip rate regardless of changes in water pressure. Water is dripped out at a specified rate, usually from 1 to 4 gallons per hour. Drip lines can be buried, but I leave mine on the surface for reassurance that they're working and so I don't inadvertently gouge them with a trowel. In areas that experience especially intense sunlight, however, exposed plastic can quickly degrade, so it's wise to bury the lines or cover them with mulch.

One way to uniformly deliver water over an area like a bed is to lay down plastic tubing with relatively close-spaced emitters along its length. As water drips from each emitter into the soil, it spreads and creates wetting fronts. If the emitters are close enough together, these wetting fronts meld together from one emitter to the next. The number of such lines needed depends on the kind of soil and the width of the bed. Clay soils have many capillary-size pores that can pull water outward about 3 feet from each point of application. The wetting front spreads about 2 feet in a silty soil and 1 foot in sandy soil.

You can purchase drip emitters to plug into inexpensive, half-inch

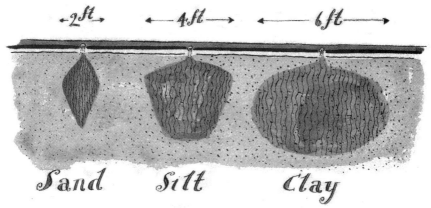

Water spread from a single drip emitter in various soil types.

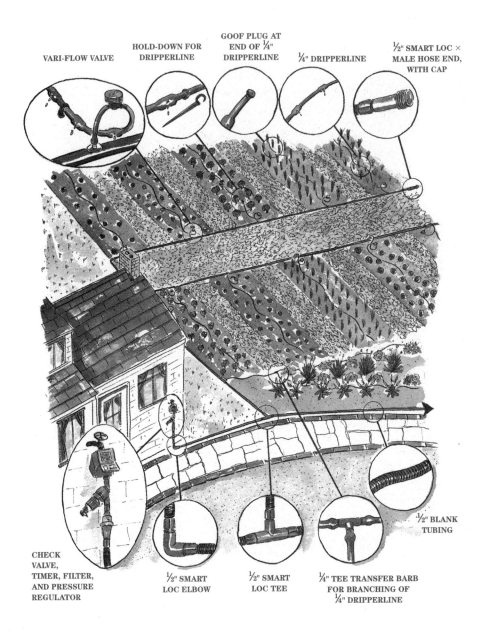

VARI-FLOW VALVE

HOLD-DOWN FOR
DRIPPERLINE

GOOF PLUG AT
END OF ¼"
DRIPPERLINE

¼" DRIPPERLINE

½" SMART LOC ×
MALE HOSE END,
WITH CAP

CHECK
VALVE,
TIMER, FILTER,
AND PRESSURE
REGULATOR

½" SMART
LOC ELBOW

½" SMART
LOC TEE

¼" TEE TRANSFER BARB
FOR BRANCHING OF
¼" DRIPPERLINE

½" BLANK
TUBING

A drip system set up to water vegetable and flower beds near a house . . .

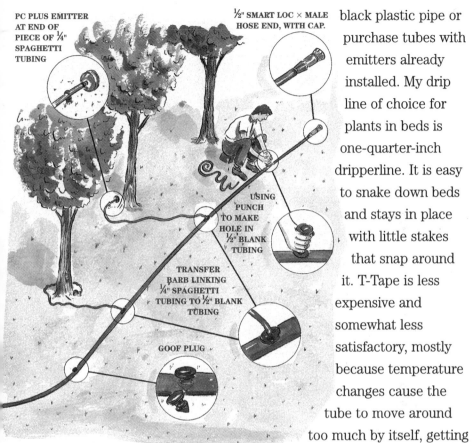

PC PLUS EMITTER AT END OF PIECE OF ¼" SPAGHETTI TUBING

½" SMART LOC × MALE HOSE END, WITH CAP.

USING PUNCH TO MAKE HOLE IN ½" BLANK TUBING

TRANSFER BARB LINKING ¼" SPAGHETTI TUBING TO ½" BLANK TUBING

GOOF PLUG

. . . and individual fruit trees farther away.

black plastic pipe or purchase tubes with emitters already installed. My drip line of choice for plants in beds is one-quarter-inch dripperline. It is easy to snake down beds and stays in place with little stakes that snap around it. T-Tape is less expensive and somewhat less satisfactory, mostly because temperature changes cause the tube to move around too much by itself, getting in the way and sometimes knocking down young plants. It also takes a bit of wrestling to attach. Pressure-compensating in-line emitter tubing is the Cadillac of drip lines, but would be overkill in my garden, which is flat and has relatively short beds that don't require the pressure-compensating feature.

Wide spacing—with a few feet between emitters or banks of emitters—is needed for irrigating trees or other widely spaced plants. I plug individual emitters, called PC Plus emitters, into half-inch plastic pipe that runs next to trees.

Microsprinklers, which are low-volume sprinklers perched atop short stakes, are another way to spread water over an area. They can be useful for ground covers or beneath older trees. Keeping leaves and stems so wet, however, can promote diseases, and sprinkling does expose the water to evaporation and blowing. Microsprinklers are best used where increased humidity is desired.

Working back from whatever drippers are in planting beds or near individual plants, we come to headers. These are the pipes—cheap, thin-walled, half- or three-quarter-inch black plastic tubing—that bring water out to the planted area. A small, inexpensive valve can be inserted between a header and any dripper or sprinkler so that water can be turned off in a particular area—when a bed is fallow or full of ripening onions, for example.

After using various L and T connectors to join header lines and work around corners, we find ourselves near the hose spigot. The first thing we come to is a pressure regulator, which reduces water pressure in the drip lines to between 5 and 20 pounds per square inch. Behind the pressure regulator is a filter to screen out particles larger than 150 or 200 microns (the amount of filtering needed depends on the particular types of emitters used). The next item is the key to convenience: a water timer that automatically turns the water on and off as specified. And the final item is a check valve, which prevents water from siphoning backward in case of a pressure drop.

Turn On

Ideally, you want water to drip into soil at exactly the rate that roots withdraw it, which occurs only during the day. Plant consumption varies with the size of the plants, the kinds of plants, the temperature,

Soaker Woes

A soaker hose may seem like the ideal way to water plants. Just lay the porous rubber hose on top of the ground, or bury it a few inches deep, turn on the faucet, and let water trickle out. One spring I did just that in my vegetable garden.

Based on the manufacturer's rating of a constant output of 1.5 gallons per hour per foot of hose, I calculated that 1 hour and 20 minutes of watering per week would keep my silty soil moist. As spring rains gave way to a drier-than-usual summer, my plants showed no signs of wilting. Then again, they didn't have the vibrancy I had expected. By season's end, I was prompted to do some testing on sections of the hose.

The ooze rate of the rubber soaker hose proved to be quite variable. Hose buried in the ground for a single season oozed less than a gallon per hour from each 1-foot section. The initial output of hose that had been in the ground but allowed to dry out was as low as 1 quart per hour. And when I tested unused sections of hose that I had left over from spring, the rate was almost 300 percent too high!

My testing was with a bucket and 1-foot sections of hose; the potential for variable output is even greater "in the field." My site is relatively flat, but if a garden has any changes in elevation, lower beds are going to get more water than upper beds. Even on flat ground, plants near the beginning of the line are going to get more water than plants near the end of the line. I say nix to soaker hoses.

the sunlight, and the wind speed among other things.

Rather than try to factor in every variable influencing the plants' water use, you could just soak the whole garden with the equivalent of a 1-inch depth of water per week, which is a good approximation of average plant water use. This amount translates to about a half gallon of water per week over each square foot of soil.

Computing how much time an emitter would take to provide that

WORKSHEET FOR DRIP IRRIGATION TIMING

PLANTS GROWING IN A UNIFORMLY WETTED BED

$$\text{MINUTES OF WATERING PER SESSION} = \frac{4.3 \times A}{B \times C \times D}$$

A = area of a bed, in square feet
B = total number of emitters in that bed
C = discharge rate for an emitter, in gallons per hour
D = number of waterings per day

	MY GARDEN*	YOUR GARDEN
A = bed area, square feet	30	
B = # emitters per bed	20	
C = emitter rate, gallons per hour	0.5	
D = # waterings per day	6	
MINUTES OF WATERING PER SESSION	2	

*One bed in my garden is 10 feet long by 3 feet wide, with one dripperline having an emitter every 6 inches running down the center of the bed. Emitters discharge ½ gallon of water per hour. Timer can turn water on and off 6 times per day.

half gallon of water per week per square foot of soil is straightforward. As an example, a silty soil watered with 1-gallon-per-hour emitters creates a wetting front around each emitter with a 4-foot-diameter circle (the wetting front spreads 2 feet from each emitter in this kind of soil). That 4-foot-diameter circle has an area of 12.5 square feet, which needs 6 gallons per week to get its needed half gallon per week per square foot of soil. At 1 gallon per hour, that emitter has to drip for six hours per week.

With drip irrigation, we want to spread that six hours of watering over as many daylight hours of the week as possible—after all, this is

INDIVIDUAL PLANTS

$$\text{MINUTES OF WATERING PER SESSION} = \frac{4.3 \times E}{F \times G \times H}$$

E = wetted area, in square feet, which is 28 for clay soils, 13 for silts, and 3 for sands
F = discharge rate for an emitter, in gallons per hour
G = number of waterings per day
H = number of emitters per plant

	MY PLANTS*	YOUR PLANTS
E = wetted area, square feet	13	
F = emitter rate, gallons per hour	0.5	
G = # waterings per day	6	
H = # emitters per plant	1	
MINUTES OF WATERING PER SESSION	20	

*This is for my fruit trees growing in a silt soil. Each tree has one emitter next to it that discharges water at the rate of 0.5 gal/hr. The timer for this system can turn the water on and off 6 times each day.

when plants drink up water. How much you can spread out that watering depends on the particular timer. My Gardena timer can be programmed to turn on and off, any day, up to six times a day, so I would divide that six hours per week over seven days to give $^6/_7$ hour of watering each day. Then I divide that $^6/_7$ hour into six waterings per day. So my water timer applies water for $^6/_7 \times ^1/_6 = ^6/_{42}$ hour, which is $^1/_7$ hour or about 9 minutes, at each of six waterings per day, at 8 A.M., 10 A.M., 12 P.M., 2 P.M., 4 P.M., and 6 P.M. For a timer that could turn the water on and off only twice each day, water would be applied for $^6/_7 \times ^1/_2 = ^6/_{14}$ or $^3/_7$ hour, which is about 27 minutes, at each of two daily

Typical Drip System for Beds and Trees

PUNCH: to put holes into half-inch blank tubing for individual emitters for trees; also to plug in transfer barbs for quarter-inch dripperline

CHECK VALVE: prevents water from siphoning back into water lines if pressure drops

WATER TIMER: a gizmo for automatically turning water on and off

FEMALE HOSE TO FEMALE PIPE ADAPTER: matches thread type between timer and filter

SPIN-CLEAN FILTER (Y-type, 150 mesh): removes particular waste from water line

PRESSURE REGULATOR (20 psi, or pounds per square inch): lowers and maintains consistent water pressure within a drip system

SMART LOC × FEMALE HOSE BEGINNING: connects blank tubing to pressure regulator

HALF-INCH BLANK TUBING: brings water to site

PREFORMED WIRE HOLD-DOWNS: keep blank tubing in place

SMART LOC ELBOWS, TEES: connectors for blank, half-inch tubing, useful for going around corners and for splitting lines in tubing

TRANSFER BARB ($1/4$"): for connecting individual emitters or emitter lines to blank tubing

QUARTER-INCH DRIPPERLINE (6" emitter spacing): for watering beds or other large areas

SUPPORT STAKES FOR DRIPPERLINE: keep quarter-inch dripperline in place

VARI-FLOW VALVES: for turning individual dripperlines on or off

PC PLUS EMITTERS ($1/2$ gph, or gallons per hour): individual emitters to plug into half-inch blank tubing

QUARTER-INCH SPAGHETTI TUBING: can carry water a short distance from each PC Plus emitter; or plug this tubing into half-inch blank tubing and terminate it with a PC Plus emitter

SMART LOC × MALE HOSE END: to close open end(s) of half-inch blank tubing

FLUSH VALVE, FEMALE HOSE THREAD: other part of closure for open end(s) of half-inch blank tubing

GOOF PLUGS: to close ends of quarter-inch dripperline, and to correct goofs (holes you punched in the wrong places)

waterings (see pages 92–93 for water schedule worksheet).

No matter how you compute watering times, when warm weather arrives, bring your check valve, timer, pressure regulator, and filter out of storage and attach them to the hose spigot and the drip irrigation line. Set the timer, turn on the water, and forget about watering until frost threatens at the other end of the season. When this time arrives, disconnect the check valve, timer, pressure regulator, and filter and put them back in storage. Plug up the beginning of the system for the winter season to keep curious creatures out of the lines. All components beyond the pressure reducer can remain outdoors through winter.

Sources for Drip Irrigation Supplies

• Dripworks
190 Sanhedrin Circle
Willits, CA 95490
800-522-3747
www.dripworksusa.com

• Gardener's Supply Co.
128 Intervale Road
Burlington, VT 05401
888-833-1412
www.gardeners.com

• The Urban Farmer Store
2833 Vicente Street
San Francisco, CA 94116
800-753-3747
www.urbanfarmerstore.com

Fine Tuning

With bare-bones treatment, drip irrigation works well enough, but the system can be fine-tuned if you want to be more conservative with water or coddle your plants a bit more.

For instance, you could lessen the time for each watering session early in the season, before plants are growing strongly and while the weather is still cool. Generally, plants need the most water when the weather is hot, windy, sunny, and/or dry.

If nothing else, you can temporarily turn off the water (just close the spigot) following a cloudburst. But have a rain gauge set up so you can measure rainfall and know when to start dripping again, and have some way of reminding yourself that the system is off. A rain sensor or a soil moisture sensor can automatically account for rainfall and plug right in to some types of water timers.

The performance of even the most automated watering system must be periodically checked. Look over your timer's shoulder to make sure the water is going on and off as planned. Then scurry over to your plants to spot-check water dripping from the emitters. Also, check the soil occasionally. Dig a hole and feel for wetness. Or insert a moisture probe, an inexpensive electronic device whose metal tip detects moisture levels. Yet another option is to install a tensiometer, a water-filled probe with a porous ceramic cup at its bottom and a dial at its top, which can be left in unfrozen ground. As always, look at your plants. Do they look happy? Are they growing well?

CHAPTER FIVE

A Cornucopia of Delectable Vegetables

Good planning and a few tricks can coax an amazing amount of high-quality vegetables from even a small garden. Planning begins with the overall layout of beds and paths and eventually narrows its focus to just where and how to plant each particular vegetable. Along the way, you might install irrigation, substitute cover crops for compost, and fine-tune your planting plans and timing to eke out the most from your plot.

Despite all that is reaped from a vegetable garden, the soil need not suffer. Even with intensive harvests, Weedless Gardening preserves or even improves the quality of the soil.

Garden Layout

Beds and paths are going to be permanent in the Weedless Garden vegetable plot, so give thought to their layout. No single design is best for every garden, but the following are some suggestions that have worked well for me and might also bring you success. For my money, a vegetable garden is easiest to manage—from planning to planting to harvest, and everything in between—if laid out in rectilinear fashion. Rectilinear does not mean ugly, just somewhat formal, with straight paths and rectangular planting beds. Any formality of my own vegetable gardens has been softened by the rustic cedar fencing surrounding them, the similar rustic cedar arbors and gates adorning the entrances, and the abutting beds of shrubs and flowers spilling out onto the lawn like flowing tidewater.

Within the vegetable garden, the primary goal is to maximize the area devoted to planting and minimize the area devoted to paths. Even though I now have enough sun-drenched, well-drained land for a spacious vegetable garden, I continue to grow my vegetables in close quarters because it makes for a smaller area to weed and mulch. Still, paths do need to be sufficiently wide for comfortable walking or wheeling about of carts and wheelbarrows full of compost and wood chips. No need to begrudge paths as merely space for travel, though, because some roots do grow beneath them.

Paths for walking can be as narrow as 12 inches wide. That is the present path width in my south vegetable garden, but I must admit that walking down these paths can make me feel like I'm being tested for driving while

A view of my vegetable garden, showing cedar fencing and dripperlines.

intoxicated. And from midsummer on, these paths become even less maneuverable as they are overhung with leaves and stems of plants growing near the edges of beds. Twelve inches is nonetheless a serviceable dimension. At the other end of the spectrum, a path wider than 24 inches is too extravagant for walking only.

As far as the width of beds is concerned, they have to be narrow enough for planting, weeding, and harvesting without having to step off the paths, yet wide enough to make efficient use of space. Unless you have the reach of a gorilla, you'll have trouble tending any bed wider than 40 inches. Narrow beds have a slight benefit over wide beds in terms of greater "edge effect." That is, plants at the edges of beds, with paths rather than plants as their neighbors on one side, experience less competition for sun and soil. A garden composed of narrow beds has more edges than the same-size garden with wide beds. On the other hand, a bed less than 30 inches wide can hardly be considered a bed

Growing Area as a Function of Bed and Path Width

These computations were made by factoring in a half-width bed located at each of two sides of the garden running parallel to the beds. These beds need to be half-width because they can be reached from only one side if the garden is fenced, as most gardens are. The reason for a bed rather than a path along the fence is so that climbing vegetables can be trained up the fence whenever they happen to be planted there.

Bed Width	Path Width	% of Garden Planted
30"	12"	40%
36"	12"	75%
36"	18"	67%
40"	12"	77%
40"	18"	69%
40"	24"	62%

at all—it's not much more than a wide row, and thus makes very inefficient use of space. Another advantage of wide beds is that they are more quickly spread with compost. Tidying the edges is what slows this job, and a garden with wide beds has fewer edges.

My north vegetable garden has 36-inch-wide beds with 18-inch-wide paths, which are dimensions I find to be a good compromise between efficiency and convenience (and are the same dimensions I'll use to make over the beds and paths in my south vegetable garden).

Long beds make the most efficient use of space, but they can also leave you muttering at having to walk their entire length and back to reach something on the other side (jump a bed and you risk landing in it). The lengths and widths for beds and paths can be varied to lay out a vegetable garden that balances efficient use of space and comfortable working dimensions.

Sky-High Beds?

For two decades, all the beds in my vegetable garden have been treated to an annual 1- to 3-inch icing of compost. Do each of these beds now stand in the garden like earthen banquet tables 20 to 60 inches high? No.

Organic materials, such as compost or wood chips, are in a continual state of decomposition. Even though compost is somewhat stabilized when ready to spread in the garden, it does continue to decompose at a slower rate.

The physical bulk that makes up compost and other organic materials comes mostly from carbon, hydrogen, and oxygen. As organic materials decompose, these elements are converted to gaseous carbon dioxide and water. Over time, a large portion of any organic material disappears, literally, into thin air.

Ground Treatment

We demand much from the soil in any vegetable garden. It must supply enough food for quick growth of vegetables and to sustain production even though nutrient-packed leaves, stems, and fruits are removed each year during harvest and cleanup. So for your annual, weed-smothering, surface-protecting mulch in the vegetable garden's beds, give the soil here the richest mulch you've got: compost.

Spreading a 1-inch layer of compost over the surface of a bed each year keeps the soil in good physical condition and generally provides all the food plants will need. With intense cropping—planting more than one vegetable in a bed each season, planting closely, and hurrying plants along with irrigation—some extra nitrogen could be needed. Late each autumn, I give my intensely cropped vegetable beds extra nitrogen by spreading 3 pounds per 100 square feet of soybean meal (see page 65). Other fertilizers also could be used, applied to give the equivalent of $2/10$ pound of actual nitrogen per 100 square feet (2 pounds of a fertilizer contains 10 percent nitrogen, for example). And fertilizer could instead be applied in late winter or early spring, before planting. (As mentioned in Chapter Three, page 48, some combination of cover crops might provide benefits equivalent to that of fertilizer and the compost blanket.)

Temporary mulches can be laid over the compost layer. This additional mulch is not a necessity, but keeps the compost layer cooler and moister—a benefit especially in hot, dry climates. Any such mulch must of course be free of weed seeds or root pieces that could awaken and start to grow. The mulch will need to be removed when it comes time to apply the next year's layer of compost. An alternative to putting down and removing this mulch would be to settle on some combination of mulch material and mulch thickness that decomposes by the time the new compost layer is needed. One such mulch that is readily available, decomposes fairly quickly, and is easy to tuck in among vegetable plants is grass clippings. In areas near water, seaweed might be available to use in this way.

Nothing special is needed for paths in the vegetable garden, except keeping them always covered with something. I use wood chips because they are readily available, free, easy to lay down, and look nice, but any of the materials for paths listed on page 26 would be suitable. All organic materials will need periodic replenishment.

Spaced-Out Plants

Forget about the instructions that you read on seed packets and in most gardening books about how far apart to plant vegetables. Those instructions are geared to conventional row planting, not bed planting. Carrot roots and leaves don't actually need 18 inches of space on either side of a row; that space is needed for a person to be able to walk alongside the row to plant, weed, and harvest.

Bed planting, right, yields more vegetables than row planting, left, and also creates a smaller area to weed.

In contrast, plants in a bed need to be no farther apart than the space necessary to keep them from fighting for sunlight, food, and water. This usually means

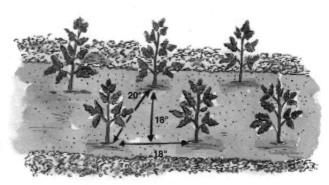

Staggered planting from one row to the next gives each tomato plant additional elbow room.

planting close enough so the leaves of each plant will eventually touch and overlap those of its neighbors on all sides. This canopy of leaves also shades out some weeds and helps shelter the soil from pelting rain and hot sun.

Bed planting gives higher yields than row planting because more of the ground is devoted to plants. With some vegetables, the size of individual vegetables decreases as yield per planted area increases. You can play around with spacing to strike some balance between total yield and size. For instance, research in England showed that onions gave the greatest yields (about 2 pounds per square foot) when planted about 2½ inches apart in all directions—but the resulting onions were only 1¼ inches in diameter. I'd rather give each of my onions more space so they're larger and need less peeling for a cookpot's worth, even at a sacrifice of total poundage. (Not much of a sacrifice really: Weedless Gardening beds yield for me over 50 pounds of onions, 3 inches or more in diameter, from a bed only 3 feet wide and 10 feet long—that's 1½ pounds per square foot.) Carrots respond differently to spacing, offering almost the same total yield over a wider range—but they are smaller at greater planting densities.

ROW SPACING FOR VARIOUS NUMBERS OF ROWS IN 36-INCH-WIDE BEDS

Number of Rows Down Bed	Inches from Edges of Bed to Outside Rows	Inches Between Rows
1	18	—
2	9	18
3	6	12
4	4.5	9
5	3.5	7

There are a few options to spacing plants in a bed. Carrots might be grown in multiple rows, each just 7 inches apart. I run rows along the length of my beds parallel to my drip irrigation lines, but short rows could be run across beds. Or carrot seeds might be scattered over a bed, then seedlings thinned to 3 inches apart in all directions. A quick way to do most of this thinning is with a garden rake teased lightly over the ground. Staked tomatoes or individual broccoli plants can run down a bed in a double row. Stagger plants from the row on one side of the bed to the other to add a little more space between them than if they sat directly across from each other.

Digging for Our Roots

In Weedless Gardening, root vegetables must be harvested while leaving the soil minimally disturbed. The procedure is actually pretty much the same as that for removing any stout-rooted weed.

With nothing more than a tug at their crowns, some root vegetables slide intact out of the soil; others need some coaxing. After oodles of compost mellow the soil over the years, you'll find roots more easily releasing their grips on the soil. When the soil is moist, almost all my carrots (even large ones) slide right out of the ground if I just pull up on them by hand. Harvest is even easier if I first slide a garden fork into the ground along each row of carrots, then push away from the plant on the handle to lift up and slightly loosen the soil. The thin, brittle roots of salsify demand such loosening, and sometimes require sliding a trowel or spade into the ground right alongside each root, then pushing the handle while pulling on the plant—like digging out a burdock weed.

Harvesting potatoes, both white and sweet, presents more of a challenge to the integrity of the soil. Admittedly, some disruption is inevitable. It can be minimized by loosening, but not inverting, the soil with a garden fork and then gingerly grubbing around for tubers by hand. If the stems are intact enough to pull on the tubers or roots, grab them for help. Again, the way you loosen the soil is by thrusting the working end of the tool into the ground, then pulling the handle toward you just enough to lift up the soil a little.

Sometimes the soil gets more than a little disrupted when digging up potatoes. It's not a catastrophe—just smooth the surface and lay on that icing of compost in preparation for the next crop.

Levering a "stuck" carrot out of the soil.

Multidimensional Vegetable Gardening

Earlier, when we formed our garden plots into beds rather than straight rows, we went beyond a single dimension. Let us now venture further into the multidimensional vegetable garden. Gardeners have dabbled here before, but the beds and good growing conditions of Weedless Gardening make it especially successful in this realm. Each added dimension brings its own benefits—in addition to increased yields.

The Layered Look

No law says that any bed or portion of a bed has to be devoted to a single vegetable at a time. Different vegetables mature at different times and take up different amounts of space, so why not commingle them together in a bed for the best use of space? Intercropping, as this technique is called, is workable with almost any combination of plants that mature at different times and spacings.

Layering or overlapping a bed of broccoli and lettuce plants is a good example of this practice. Two lettuce plants spaced 8 inches apart can live between broccoli plants spaced 2 feet apart. This system makes better use of space than giving lettuce and broccoli each their own beds, with all that space between broccoli plants bare until neighboring leaves finally touch. The lettuce is

Broccoli, lettuce, and radishes sharing a single bed.

harvested and out of the way by the time the broccoli plants finally fill the bed.

No need to restrict intercropping to just two different vegetables at a time. Run a long row of spring radishes up the center of that same bed of broccoli and lettuce (or just squeeze it in, in short rows here and there) and you have three layers of plantings in one bed. The radishes are harvested and out of the way before the lettuces fill in, and they are out of the way before the broccolis fill in.

Besides putting more vegetables into your mouth, intercropping helps put less into the mouths of insect pests. Many pests that fly or crawl around looking for food become confused by the mixed sensory signals from a mixed bed of vegetables. It is much easier to hone in on a solid stand of cabbages than cabbages mixed in with tomato or bean plants, for example.

The combinations of vegetables that can rub elbows are almost endless, so experiment to find the ones that work best in your climate and with your bed sizes. In addition to the previously mentioned mix of broccoli, lettuce, and radish plants, other vegetable marriages that work well for me are early cabbage, lettuce, and onion sets; lettuce transplants with pole beans; staked tomatoes with lettuce; and peppers with carrots. Radishes and carrots are a traditional interplant, with the radishes widely spaced along the row not only providing crunchy roots to precede the carrots but also marking the row where slow-to-emerge carrot seedlings will eventually appear.

The most famous interplant combination is the "Three Sisters." The name was given by Native Americans to corn, beans, and squash (or pumpkins) because these three vegetables provided such a large degree of sustenance. Corn and bean seeds were planted on small mounds of soil fertilized with wood ashes and animal offal, and pumpkins were sown between these mounds. It was a congenial association; the beans enriched the soil with nitrogen they took from the air; corn plants acted as stakes upon which the beans could clamber; and the pumpkins vines strewed their large leaves over the ground to shade out weeds.

The traditional Three Sisters planting involved field corn, dry pole beans, and winter squash or pumpkin, all of which are harvested at the end of the season. Today's

A modern Three Sisters planting of winter squash, kidney beans, and popcorn.

gardeners are more apt to grow sweet corn, green beans, and summer squashes. The problem is that such a planting will have modern gardeners stepping on squashes as they fight through scratchy squash leaves, and having to uncurl bean vines from around ears of ripe corn.

My suggestion for a modern Three Sisters planting is to plan for a one-time, end-of-the-season harvest of winter squash, dry beans (kidney, for example) and—with a nod to modern palates and kitchens—popcorn (which Native Americans also grew).

3-D: Growing Up

"Grow up" is what I tell some of the vegetables in my beds, and when they do, a third dimension is added to the growing space. Peas, cucumbers, melons, tomatoes, and other vining plants can be planted close together or allowed to mingle more closely with other vegetables when grown on a trellis or a stake. The result: more food per square foot of planted ground.

Another plus for vegetables trained upward is that they stay cleaner than their ground-dwelling counterparts. Bathing in air and basking in sunlight also allows fruits and foliage of upright plants to dry quickly, cutting down on disease problems. And succulent fruits, such as tomatoes and melons, that are grown off the ground are less likely to be reached and attacked by slugs and turtles.

Some plants cry out to be staked while others are more ambivalent. The stems of twining plants such as pole beans, or of plants with tendrils such as peas and cucumbers, flounder about looking for some support; once they find it, they will naturally pull themselves up. Not so for tomato vines. With long stems but no means for clinging, tomato plants are as happy to crawl over the ground as to climb a stake, so they need to be tied or otherwise helped up.

Both natural and manufactured materials are suitable for stakes or trellises. Regardless of staking material, avoid root damage by pushing or pounding stakes into the ground before or when you plant seeds or set out transplants. If a plant needs to be tied to a stake, avoid harmful rubbing by using a thick or soft material, such as rag strips or soft, thick string. Tie the material first firmly to the stake to prevent slippage, then only loosely around the plant's stem.

Size the stake to the plant. Tomato plants are lusty growers and heavy once weighted down

Staking possibilities: bamboo, wood, heavy wire, metal pipe.

with fruits, so they need a stake with at least the muscle of 2" × 2" lumber or five-eighth-inch metal pipe. Electrical-conduit pipe makes stakes that are inexpensive and easy to pound into the ground. If the appearance of bare metal offends you, purchase metal stakes painted green to look like bamboo, or simply use real bamboo. Pole beans can be supported on three-quarter-inch bamboo, and in fact, should not be given any stake thicker than this or the vines will have trouble twining around it to climb. You can get around having to poke the base of bamboo stakes deep into the ground by joining the tops of three or four of them into a self-supporting tepee. Other possibilities for staking are commercially available spiral metal stakes that contain a growing stem, and straight stems from pruning shrubs and trees.

Multi-stemmed twiggy prunings are excellent for trellising. Push their bases into the soil, line them up close together in the plant row, then cut back any branches oriented perpendicularly to the row so there is a single plane of twiggy branches. Other possibilities for trellising are chicken wire (poultry netting) and wide-mesh string netting. Or make your own string trellis for vines to climb, using string that is cotton or another natural material so that eventually it can be tossed into the compost pile along with the attached vines.

Wire cages (1- to 2-foot cylinders of sturdy wire with large

Twiggy prunings make a lightweight trellis for peas.

The Almost Ultimate Trellis

Twiggy prunings make a charming trellis and are especially suitable for a delicate climber like peas. Such a trellis, however, demands plenty of a certain type of pruning and a hefty investment in preparation time, and it will never be strong enough to support robust-growing or heavy-fruited vegetables.

Here is my less charming but more serviceable solution. The first step is to pound a 5-foot length of old, inch-thick iron plumbing pipe (obtained free from the recycling center) into the ground at the center of each row end. The trellis material is 2-inch-mesh chicken wire, 4 feet high. The easiest way to attach it to the pipes is to open just the end of the roll of chicken wire and weave it partway onto one pipe. Next, walk down the row, unrolling the chicken wire as you go, then weave it partway onto the pipe at the other end. The chicken wire slides down the pipes most easily if kept almost par-

My "almost ultimate" pea trellis.

allel to the ground. (I scurry back and forth, easing the mesh down to the ground as I weave it onto the pipes.) Once the chicken wire is at ground level, it can be cut to the length of the row, or the excess roll can be just left standing against the pipe.

At this point, the trellis is quite floppy. Strengthen it with posts (such as the inexpensive fiberglass types sold for electric fencing) woven into the chicken wire and pushed into the ground every 3 feet or so. Handle the posts with gloved hands to avoid getting fiberglass shards in your skin.

Presto! In about 15 minutes you can have a sturdy trellis. It can be put up after plants emerge through the soil, and makes up for any initial lack of charm by spending only a short time bare of a leafy covering. After harvest, pull the vines off the trellis and take it down in a reversal of the previous steps. Because it's not permanent, you can move it around the garden to a different location each spring—just as you should your vegetables.

openings) function like stakes or trellises. I train some of my tomato plants to grow up the middle of 5-foot-tall cylinders I make from 6-inch-mesh concrete reinforcement wire. At the base of other such cylinders, I plant melons or cucumbers, which (once I help their vines to grab onto the metal wire) pull themselves up.

No matter what kind of trellis is used for a melon, the fruit needs to be supported in some sort of hammock or it will either drop or pull the vine down. Mesh bags in which onions or oranges are sold, old pantyhose, or old, torn bird netting all make suitable hammocks that can be clipped to a trellis with clothespins.

As you become more familiar with this third dimension in gardening, you can begin to integrate it into your two-dimensional techniques. Play around with different combinations, always giving plants enough space to bask in the sun and develop. Some combinations that have worked well in my beds have been trellised cucumbers growing between late plantings of broccoli and kale. Earlier in the season, that same trellis lets my peas keep close company with lettuce and onions. I've also kept lettuce, which hates hot weather, growing happily into summer by planting it in the dappled shade cast by cucumbers on an inclined trellis. Wire cages let early lettuce, then basil, grow at the feet of my tomato vines, which eventually become columns of green, each only 18 inches from its neighbor.

This trellis provides support for cucumbers and shade for lettuce.

The Fourth Dimension

The fourth dimension in the Weedless Garden is time. Few vegetables are in the ground from the very beginning to the very end of the growing season, even where spring frost lingers late and autumn frost arrives early. There's often time to slip two—even three— different vegetables into the same piece of ground in one season.

Succession planting, as the technique is called, also spreads out the harvest. Bush beans typically yield well for two to four weeks; two or three sowings, the last one in midsummer, yield a continuous supply. (In practice, it's better to avoid pest buildup by locating successive plantings of the same vegetable in different parts of the garden.)

Filling the time slots for succession planting is like doing a puzzle. For instance, tomato plants cannot go into the ground until the weather warms, so why not plant and harvest a crop of spinach, which thrives in cool weather, before the tomatoes? Bush beans that peter out by midsummer can be followed by cabbage. I have successfully followed early beets with late bush beans (or vice versa), or early lettuce with bush beans followed by late radishes. Sweet corn allows enough time even this far north, from sowing to ripening, to precede or follow it with turnips, radishes, spinach, or something else that matures quickly. I can even precede corn with peas—if the corn is a short-season variety. Alternately, when summer heat turns pea pods tough, I might pull the pea vines and plant carrots for autumn harvest in their place.

Moving part of the succession out of the garden is another time trick. Pre-sprouting seeds in moist paper towels lets ground outdoors be used for a few extra days until the seeds sprout. Making use of transplants, which are sown and then spend their youth in small containers, is another way to cheat time. Buy or grow your own transplants and reap two benefits: The plants spend their first weeks huddled together, taking up an insignificant amount of space, and you can have other vegetables growing out in the garden while seedlings are growing to transplant size.

Lettuce is a good example of a vegetable that can yield abundantly, even in a small garden, especially if transplanted. By using small plastic seed flats that each hold either 6 or 12 plants, a mere square foot of space can house 25 or more seedlings. Alternatively, a nursery area can even be set right out in the garden for growing transplants; again, only a small area is needed. The first lettuces I harvest grow right where I will later plant heat lovers such as tomato, pepper, eggplant, cucumber, melon, and okra. Lettuce sown in containers from midsummer on is ideal for transplanting at the other end of the growing season. Just pop lettuce transplants into the ground as soon as space becomes available, perhaps where spent bush beans or corn plants have been cleared away, or onions harvested.

Cabbage, broccoli, endive, and Chinese cabbage take longer to mature than lettuce, but can similarly be slipped into the garden at the beginning or end of the season.

With succession planting, the garden bears much more than just the typical summer harvest. The bounty of spring and autumn become as significant as that of summer—it's almost like having a whole new garden or two! Rather than the melancholy sight of dying tomato and pepper plants, the autumn garden offers kale, broccoli, lettuce, radishes, and endive. The only stumbling block to creating this lush autumn tableau is that planning and planting must be done in summer, which, unlike spring, does not bring on primal urges for planting. Summer planting is a purely rational act.

A Fifth Dimension?

Is it possible to find yet another dimension in the vegetable garden, a dimension beyond space and time? Well, sort of. The fifth dimension is made up of a few tricks designed to find time where it is not, tricks meant to add days or weeks to the beginning and/or end of the growing season. This translates to a longer harvest season, and with plants blanketing the ground more of the year, more soil improvement from the top down.

• **WARMING THE SOIL:** Even when the air is balmy in late winter or early spring, cold soil can delay planting. It can also delay sprouting of seeds, during which time they are apt to rot or be eaten by animals. How cold is "too cold" depends on the particular type of seed; each has its own minimum germination temperature. Transplants plopped into soil that is too cold are apt to sulk rather than grow, with rot settling into their roots. A soil thermometer with a long metal probe comes in handy for telling when and what to plant in spring.

Soil temperatures lag behind air temperatures in spring because more heat is needed to warm soil particles and water than air. Dry soil warms up faster than wet soil, so raised beds, which have good water drainage and increased surface exposure to the air, warm up faster than flat or sunken beds. Quicker soil warming does not necessarily justify raised beds in itself, except perhaps where growing seasons are so short that every extra growing day is precious. And quick-drying raised beds are not nearly so appealing in midsummer, when water might become limited.

No need to twiddle your thumbs waiting for the soil to warm in spring. In the Weedless Garden, you may have already done one thing to warm the soil—spread compost, the dark color of which captures the sun's heat. Then again, you also may have grown a winter cover crop. Dead or alive, cover crops insulate the soil, retarding the soil's warming in spring (and delaying cooling in autumn). In cool weather, remove any cover crop from a bed two weeks before the bed is to be planted.

Any mulch other than compost that was laid on a bed during the previous season, but has not decomposed by planting time, is similarly going to insulate the soil. To hasten warming and make way for planting, remove mulch to the compost pile or to the paths between the beds.

• **WARMING THE AIR:** Cold air also delays planting at the beginning of the season and can cut the harvest short at the other end. A way to warm the air (and hence, the soil) at either end of the growing season—essentially to "move" your garden to a warmer climate—is with cloches (French for "bell"). The original cloches were large glass bell jars that French market gardeners temporarily set over plants to act as miniature greenhouses. At one time, acres and acres of bell jar–covered fields surrounded Paris and supplied out-of-season vegetables to the city's households and restaurants.

Traditional cloches had limitations. With little interior volume, the air inside could quickly heat up on a sunny day, possibly to the point of killing plants within. A professional gardening friend of mine,

Plastic cloche   *Hotkap*   *Wall O' Water*   *Tunnel cloche*

trained in France, tells of trudging out to cloche-covered fields on bright, frosty mornings to slide a block of wood under one side of each cloche, then returning in late afternoon to kick out each block. Count off-season storage, weight, cost, and potential breakage among other limitations of those traditional cloches.

Fortunately, the cloche has been modernized. A Hotkap, for example, is a wax-paper hat that you place over a plant and anchor with soil on its brim. A gallon plastic milk jug with its bottom cut off can lead a useful afterlife as a cloche, as can a glass jug whose bottom has been lopped off with a bottle cutter. Newer types of cloches, such as tepees of water-filled tubes (Wall O' Water), fiberglass or plastic boxes and A-frames, and even bell jars (back again, of glass or plastic), are always coming on the market.

The need to contain heat by night and yet not overheat by day makes air leakage a tricky proposition with the design of any cloche. Personally, I forgo some heat retention for the luxury of less bother with venting. Vent Hotkaps by tearing the wax paper progressively more open as the season advances, and homemade jug cloches by unscrewing their caps. Some kinds of cloches are most easily vented with the traditional block of wood lifting a corner, which is not so bad if you don't have to vent a whole field of them.

Structurally, so-called floating row covers go far beyond the bell jar, but they have the same function—to temporarily protect plants out in the garden. In fact, floating row covers are structureless; they are lightweight, woven or spun bonded fabrics that drape loosely over plants to "float up" with growing leaves and stems. A single piece of row cover can be draped over an entire bed; sunlight, rain, and sprays pass right through. The temperature under floating row covers holds at only about 6°F higher than the temperature outside, but no venting is needed.

Sources for Cloches

- Garden City Seeds, P.O. Box 204, Thorp, WA 98946, 509-964-7000, www.gardencityseeds.com

- Gardener's Supply Co., 128 Intervale Road, Burlington, VT 05401, 888-833-1412, www.gardeners.com

- Johnny's Selected Seeds, 1 Foss Hill Road, R.R. 1, Box 2580, Albion, ME 04910, 207-437-9294, www.johnnyseeds.com

- Kinsman Company, P.O. Box 428, Point Pleasant, PA 18950, 800-733-4146, www.kinsmangarden.com

- Mellinger's, Inc., 2310 West South Range Road, North Lima, OH 44452, 800-321-7444, www.mellingers.com

- Nichols Garden Nursery, 1190 Old Salem Road NE, Albany, OR 97321, 541-928-9280, www.nicholsgardennursery.com

Another convenient way to protect a whole bed of plants is with some sort of continuous tunnel cloche. A tunnel cloche is like a long, miniature greenhouse. The temperature of the larger volume of air underneath does not plunge as low at night, nor soar as high on sunny days, as compared to individual cloches.

A tunnel cloche might consist of clear-paned tent- or barn-shaped structures with open ends set end-to-end down the length of a planting bed. A vertical pane held in place with a stake at each end of the tunnel seals it closed. Garden planning helps make most efficient use of such cloches. I grow an early warm-season crop in a bed adjacent to where I grow an early cool-season crop. So the same cloches that protect and speed along lettuce, cabbage, or spinach in the "cool" bed then need to be lifted only one bed over when it comes time to start early bush beans, sweet corn, or some other warm-season crop. When I bring my cloches out again at the end of the growing season, I first put them over cold-weather crops, such as lettuce and Chinese cabbage, that offer a single harvest and tolerate moderate amounts of cold. In an adjacent bed, I'll grow spinach, mâche, and other vegetables that survive and offer harvest the whole winter when I move the cloches over them.

Another form of modern tunnel cloche consists of clear plastic film held aloft by a series of metal or plastic hoops anchored in place with their ends poked into the soil. A second set of hoops, placed

Floating row cover and plastic tunnel over separate beds.

over the first and with the plastic sandwiched between, keeps the plastic in place and allows it to be slid up for venting or harvesting. Alternately, the plastic might be attached to single hoops with specialized clips. At each end of the tunnel, the plastic is gathered together, tied, and staked.

As long as we're putting hoops of clear plastic over the garden, why not cobble together or purchase something a little larger, something large enough to walk into? Like a greenhouse. Some variations on the standard greenhouse theme include greenhouses whose coverings are easily removed in late spring, then replaced in late summer, and greenhouses that slide back and forth in the garden, alternately protecting cold-tolerant vegetables in frigid weather and heat-loving vegetables in cool weather. The plants and soil in such cloche-like greenhouses benefit from exposure to ambient sun, rain, and wind when cold protection is not needed. Depending on the structure, your climate, what you grow, and whether or not you opt to supplement heat from the sun, a small greenhouse could close the harvest season's loop between late autumn and early spring.

Trying to fill every available niche of physical space and time in the vegetable garden is like doing a multidimensional jigsaw puzzle. Assembling this puzzle can sometimes bring on as much frustration as doing a real jigsaw puzzle. Don't get overwrought trying to integrate every "puzzle piece" into every square inch of garden; when in doubt, just go ahead and plant. Keep records as you play with your puzzle, though, or you're sure to repeat some failures as well as forget some successes.

"Nothing puzzles me more than time and space; and yet nothing troubles me less, as I never think of them," wrote Charles Lamb 200 years ago. Not so for us Weedless Vegetable Gardeners.

Vegetables on Parade

What follows is not a comprehensive treatise on growing vegetables, but specific guidelines for growing vegetables in Weedless Gardening. I have also thrown in a few extra tidbits here and there, such as the names of particularly favorite vegetable varieties. There's room for fine-tuning much of the information on spacing, always taking into account the fertility of your soil and whether or not you are irrigating. Most of these figures reflect my own growing experiences, with very fertile soil and drip irrigation, seasoned with what I have gleaned from various literature, including (yes!) instructions on seed packets.

Beds for the examples that follow are 36 inches wide (see page 99 for row-spacing parameters). To adapt the recommendations to other beds, multiply my within-row plant-spacing recommendations by the between-row spacing to get square inches per plant, which you can then translate to other rows.

Within each vegetable entry, SEASON refers to the usual growing and harvest times (see the worksheet on pages 122–125 for planting dates for specific vegetables). TRANSPLANT indicates whether the particular vegetable is typically transplanted or direct-seeded right into the garden. Theoretically, any vegetable could be transplanted, but some don't yield enough per plant to justify transplanting (peas, for example), and others are too easily disrupted by the operation (parsnips). The DAYS TO MATURITY listing for each entry is a rough guide. Cool or warm weather will slow down or speed up the process, respectively, and some varieties will mature beyond the range offered.

Sources for Vegetable Seeds

- Fedco Seeds, P.O. Box 520
  Waterville, MA 04903
  207-873-7333
  www.fedcoseeds.com

- Johnny's Selected Seeds
  1 Foss Hill Road
  R.R. 1, Box 2580
  Albion, ME 04910, 207-437-9294
  www.johnnyseeds.com

- J. W. Jung Seed Company
  335 South High Street
  Randolph, WI 53957
  800-297-3123, www.jungseed.com

- Nichols Garden Nursery
  1190 Old Salem Road NE
  Albany, OR 97321
  541-928-9280
  www.nicholsgardennursery.com

- Redwood City Seed Co.
  P.O. Box 361
  Redwood City, CA 94064
  650-325-7333
  www.batnet.com/rwc-seed/

- Seed Savers Exchange
  3076 North Winn Road
  Decorah, IA 52101
  319-382-5990, www.seedsavers.org

PLANTING DATES FOR VEGETABLES

*Your average last spring frost and first fall frost dates can
be obtained from your local Cooperative Extension Service.*

	AVERAGE SPRING FROST DATE = 0	AVERAGE FALL FROST DATE = 0	MY GARDEN AVERAGE SPRING FROST DATE IS *May 21*
VEGETABLE	NUMBER OF WEEKS TO SOWING DATE	NUMBER OF WEEKS TO SOWING DATE	EARLIEST CROP
Arugula	-6	-6	*April 7*
Asparagus	*(perennial)*	*(perennial)*	—
Beans	-1	-12 *(bush)*	*May 15*
Beets	-4	-12	*April 21*
Broccoli	-9•	-12	*March 15*
Brussels sprouts	-9•	—	*March 15*
Cabbage	-9•	-12	*March 15*
Carrot	-4	12	*April 21*
Cauliflower	-7•	-12	*March 21*
Celery, celeriac	-12•	—	*February 21*
Chinese cabbage	*(varies)*	*(varies)*	*(varies)*
Corn	-1	-14	*May 15*
Cucumber	-4•••	-12	*April 21*
Eggplant	-7••••	—	*April 1*
Endive, escarole	-9•••	-12	*March 15*
Garlic	—	-5	*August 15*
Kale	-9•	-12	*March 15*
Kohlrabi	-3	-12	*May 1*
Leek	-15••••	—	*February 1*

KEY

- Indoors, for transplanting outdoors 6 weeks later
- • Indoors, for transplanting outdoors 11 weeks later
- • • Indoors, for transplanting outdoors 4 weeks later
- • • • Indoors, for transplanting outdoors 8 weeks later

YOUR GARDEN

AVERAGE FALL FROST DATE IS October 1	AVERAGE SPRING FROST DATE IS ___	AVERAGE FALL FROST DATE IS ___
LATEST CROP	**EARLIEST CROP**	**LATEST CROP**
August 15		
—		
July 1		
July 1		
July 1		
—		
July 1		
July 1		
July 1		
—		
(varies)		
June 15		
July 1		
—		
July 1		
—		
July 1		
July 1		
—		

PLANTING DATES FOR VEGETABLES *continued*

			MY GARDEN
	AVERAGE SPRING FROST DATE = 0	**AVERAGE** FALL FROST DATE = 0	**AVERAGE** SPRING FROST DATE IS *May 21*
VEGETABLE	**NUMBER OF WEEKS TO SOWING DATE**	**NUMBER OF WEEKS TO SOWING DATE**	**EARLIEST CROP**
Lettuce	-9•••	-6	*March 15*
Mâche	-7	-4	*April 1*
Melon	-4•••	—	*April 21*
Mustard	-6	-6	*April 15*
Okra	1	—	*June 1*
Onion, from plants	-15••••	—	*February 1*
Onion, from sets	-5	—	*April 15*
Parsley	-9••••	-12	*March 15*
Parsnip	-4	—	*April 21*
Peas	-7	—	*April 1*
Pepper	-7••••	—	*April 1*
Potato, white	-5	-14	*April 15*
Radish	-7	*(varies)*	*April 1*
Rutabaga	-2	-11	*May 7*
Salsify	-4	—	*April 21*
Spinach	-6	-6	*April 15*
Squash	0	-12	*May 21*
Sweet potato	1	—	*June 1*
Swiss chard	-5	–11	*April 15*
Tomato	-7••••	—	*April 1*
Turnip	-5	-6	*April 15*

YOUR GARDEN

AVERAGE FALL FROST DATE IS *October 1*	AVERAGE SPRING FROST DATE IS ————	AVERAGE FALL FROST DATE IS ————
LATEST CROP	**EARLIEST CROP**	**LATEST CROP**
August 15		
September 1		
—		
August 15		
—		
—		
—		
July 1		
—		
—		
—		
June 15		
(varies)		
July 7		
—		
August 15		
July 1		
—		
July 7		
—		
August 15		

Asparagus

SEASON: Perennial, with harvest period each spring.

TRANSPLANT: Planting asparagus "crowns" (roots) allows for a year's jump on the first harvest.

DAYS TO MATURITY: Light harvest two years after planting crowns, three years after planting seeds.

COMMENTS: Forget about the usual directives to excavate deep trenches when planting one- or two-year-old crowns of asparagus. Purchase the crowns, then dig holes wide enough to fan them out but no deeper than necessary to cover them.

After you plant, blanket the ground with 2 to 4 inches of mulch. Full harvest begins three to four years after planting and lasts about six weeks each spring and early summer for 50 or more years.

Asparagus is well worth growing. Its fresh flavor is different—and far better—than that found in any variety you could buy off the shelf. Asparagus is also decorative, doesn't need irrigation (except perhaps in arid climates), and is not eaten by

Asparagus's ferny foliage provides a verdant background for flowers.

rabbits, woodchucks, or deer. Spaced 12 to 18 inches apart, it makes a ferny backdrop for a flower bed. Keep mulched year-round with any organic material.

Beans, Snap and Lima

SEASON: Warm.

TRANSPLANT: No.

DAYS TO MATURITY: 50–70 days for snap beans, 65–90 days for lima beans; for either snap or lima beans, pole types take longer to mature than bush types.

COMMENTS: Sow bush types about 2 inches apart in the row, with the first planting on the last spring frost date for your area. (To find out the average date of the last spring frost, call your local Cooperative Extension Service or ask at the local plant nursery.) I run two rows up each bed, flanking a row of lettuce, spinach, or some other quicker cool-weather crop that is harvested and out of the way by the time the beans fill in the middle of the bed. Repeated plantings provide nonstop beans.

Give pole varieties one pole per plant, or grow them on a trellis running up the middle of a bed with seeds spaced 3 inches apart. Leafy vegetables growing beneath poled pole beans appreciate the shade as temperatures turn sultry. Pole beans start bearing later than bush beans, but a single planting keeps pumping out beans the whole season.

'King of the Garden' is a delectable pole lima bean. 'Kentucky Wonder' is a tasty pole snap bean, and 'Romano,' pole or bush, is a delicious Italian-type bean. 'Scarlet Runner' makes fat, hairy, ugly beans, but they taste good and follow on the heels of traffic-stopping scarlet flowers. My all-around favorite snap bean for fresh eating and freezing is 'Blue Lake,' pole or bush.

Beans, Soy

SEASON: Warm.

TRANSPLANT: No.

DAYS TO MATURITY: 75–90 days.

COMMENTS: Forget about tofu, tempeh, plastic, and everything else into which soybeans can be processed. This heading is concerned only with vegetable soybeans (called edamame in Japan) that you harvest green, steam or boil for several minutes, then pop out of their shells and into your mouth. The taste combines the best of fresh peas and lima beans. Plant soybeans on the last spring frost date, sowing every 2 inches, with two rows per bed. Plants are bushy but floppy, so I hold them up with twine strung between stakes I put along the edges and at the corners of the beds.

Beets

SEASON: Cool or warm.
TRANSPLANT: No.
DAYS TO MATURITY: 50–60 days.
COMMENTS: Beets are not one of my favorite vegetables, so rather than fill up a whole bed or even a portion of one with beets, I run a single row all or partway down one side. Each plant needs about 36 square inches, so if you are a beet fanatic, run five rows down each bed and eventually thin to a 5-inch spacing.

Each beet "seed" is a fruit that gives rise to more than one plant—so thin beets ruthlessly to prevent overcrowding. Many gardeners love to eat the thinnings as baby beet greens.

Broccoli

SEASON: Cool, but an early sowing will yield all summer with good growing conditions.
TRANSPLANT: Yes; grow for about six weeks before planting out.
DAYS TO MATURITY: 45–70 days from transplanting.
COMMENTS: I set two rows of transplants down the beds in early spring, with plants spaced 18 inches apart. Although the rows are 20 inches apart, staggering plants from one row to the next puts each 22 inches, diagonally, from its neighbor in the next row.

Just in case the spring crop peters out, I sow a second crop about three months before the average date of the first fall frost—early summer in the Northeast.

Brussels Sprouts

SEASON: Sow in early spring to grow all summer for harvest in cool autumn weather.

TRANSPLANT: Yes; grow for about six weeks before planting out.

DAYS TO MATURITY: 100–110 days from transplanting.

COMMENTS: Just like broccoli, plant two rows of transplants down each bed in early spring, with plants spaced 18 inches apart. These plants require a full growing season, from spring through fall, before harvest begins. I stake Brussels sprouts to keep plants tidy and the sprouts clean.

Brussels sprouts are among the best cold-hardy vegetables; I harvest right into early winter. A harvest that lasts through the winter is possible where winters are mild.

Cabbage

SEASON: Cool, but they will yield all summer with good growing conditions.

TRANSPLANT: Yes; grow for about six weeks before planting out.

DAYS TO MATURITY: 60–110 days after transplanting.

COMMENTS: Cabbage can be grown with the same spacing as broccoli. However, I prefer fairly small, meal-size cabbage heads, which I get by squeezing them even closer together. Three rows in a bed, with plants spaced 12 inches apart in each row and staggered from one row to the next, gives about 150 square inches per plant. Rather than plant solid blocks or rows of cabbage, I sneak in transplants here and there, as space becomes available, for an autumn crop. 'Early Jersey Wakefield,' dating back to the 1840s, is a variety worthy of veneration and the only one I grow.

Carrots

SEASON: Cool; sow in early spring for early summer harvest, or in summer for an even tastier harvest during cool autumn weather.
TRANSPLANT: No.
DAYS TO MATURITY: 55–75 days.
COMMENTS: A 36-inch bed can accommodate three, four, or five rows of carrots thinned to 1 to 2 inches apart, depending on the size of root desired. 'Scarlet Nantes' is an old, flavorful variety.

I grow carrots only for autumn harvest. I'd rather eat tomatoes, cucumbers, and the like in summer. Carrots also taste better in autumn, and late plantings pretty much avoid carrot rust flies.

Cauliflower

SEASON: Cool; sow in early spring for early summer harvest, or in summer for an even tastier harvest during cool autumn weather.
TRANSPLANT: Yes; grow for about six weeks before planting out.
DAYS TO MATURITY: 50–60 days after transplanting.
COMMENTS: Grow cauliflower just like broccoli and cabbage, except plant them out a bit later in spring because cauliflower is more frost-tender. For individual-size portions ("mini-caulis" are what they're called in Britain), plant at 6" × 6" spacings instead. 'Violet Queen' is an excellent variety of purple cauliflower that turns green after being cooked.

I prefer to grow cauliflower for autumn harvest. With cool weather, ripe heads can stay on the plant in good condition. An early summer sowing that spends its first six weeks in containers can be tucked into the garden randomly as these plants make few demands for space.

Celery and Celeriac

SEASON: Cool, but they will yield all summer with good growing conditions.

TRANSPLANT: Yes; grow for 10–12 weeks before planting out.

DAYS TO MATURITY: 100–120 days after transplanting.

COMMENTS: Plant two rows of either vegetable (celeriac has a swollen, edible root) in a 36-inch bed with plants spaced 8 inches apart. Fertile, constantly moist soil with plenty of humus is a must for celery.

Ignore any advice about "hilling up" celery stalks or wrapping them in paper to blanche them and make them more tender; the practice went out of vogue years ago. Also bypass 'Golden Self Blanching,' even though it does blanch all by itself. Instead try 'Ventura,' which is green and tasty.

Chinese Cabbage

SEASON: Cool.

TRANSPLANT: Yes; grow for 4–6 weeks before planting out, or direct-seed.

DAYS TO MATURITY: 40–70 days after transplanting.

COMMENTS: Chinese cabbages come in an assortment of types and sizes, so spacing in beds depends on variety. I grow them mostly as an autumn crop, because short springs and hot summers here cause them to bolt (flower) too soon as a spring crop. 'Mei Qing' is quick maturing and makes small, manageable heads that can be grown as close as 8 inches apart in all directions.

Corn

SEASON: Warm.

TRANSPLANT: No.

DAYS TO MATURITY: 65–95 days.

COMMENTS: Some people contend that it doesn't pay to grow sweet corn in the garden because it takes up too much space and it's inexpensive to buy. But you just cannot buy the very tastiest—and freshest—corn at the market. 'Golden Bantam,' for example, is a variety that dates back to 1906 and has a flavor that is sweet and rich but not cloying.

Plant corn in hills, with two rows of hills per bed and 18 inches between hills within each row. A hill is not a mound of soil but rather a station—a place where you plant a clump of seeds, six to eight in the case of sweet corn. Thin each hill to the sturdiest three to four plants after they're up and growing. Yields are an ear or two per square foot of bed, which is not bad if you consider that the planting bed could also used for other vegetables, earlier and later in the season.

Cucumber

SEASON: Warm

TRANSPLANT: Not necessary, but sowing indoors one month early results in an extra-early crop.

Clumps, or "hills," of corn planted in two staggered rows down a bed.

DAYS TO MATURITY: 45–60 days.

COMMENTS: Plant cucumber seeds or transplants into warm soil every 18 inches down the middle of your beds, but be prepared to keep moving errant stems off paths. If the prospect of this bothers you, plant a short-vined variety like 'Bush Crop' or 'Salad Bush.' Even better, plant cukes a foot apart, 6 inches in from the edge of the bed, then train the vines up a trellis inclined over the bed. Below it, you can grow a shade-tolerant and heat-hating vegetable such as lettuce or spinach.

Cucumbers do eventually succumb to pests, so I make a second sowing about six weeks after the first. This keeps me awash in cucumbers all summer. My favorite varieties include 'Suyo Long' and 'Amira' for flavor and tenderness, and 'County Fair' for reliability. Also, try pickling types for delicious fresh eating.

Eggplant

SEASON: Warm.

TRANSPLANT: Yes; grow for about eight weeks before planting out.

DAYS TO MATURITY: 60–75 days after transplanting.

COMMENTS: Transplant seedlings after frost has reliably passed, in two rows with plants spaced 18 to 24 inches apart.

Eggplants come in a varieties of shapes, sizes, and colors, including white of course. Particularly dependable and tasty is the hybrid variety 'Ichiban.'

Endive and Escarole

SEASON: Cool.

TRANSPLANT: Yes; grow for about four weeks before planting out.

DAYS TO MATURITY: 45 days after transplanting.

COMMENTS: Plant three rows of either vegetable in a 36-inch bed with

10 inches between plants. Start some seedlings in flats in midsummer, then transplant them to their own bed or among waning summer vegetables. The crisp days of autumn bring out the best in endive and escarole. To make their leaves look and taste more delicate, blanche them by inverting a clay flowerpot over the whole plant or by bunching and holding the leaves together with a rubber band. Or do nothing: Usually the heads grow so thick with leaves that they blanche many of the inner ones without any help from me.

Garlic

SEASON: Grows through year; ripens in late summer.
TRANSPLANT: Plant cloves.
DAYS TO MATURITY: 11 months.
COMMENTS: Plant in late summer, putting five rows of cloves down a bed with cloves spaced about 6 inches apart in each row. It's commonly recommended to plant garlic in late fall, but when cloves are planted earlier, they establish more roots before growth is arrested by the cold. An abundance of roots keep the plants well anchored into the soil through winter, and can fuel more growth next spring. Harvest garlic in summer when lower leaves start to yellow. Sort through the bulbs after harvest and stick some individual cloves right back into the ground in late August or early September.

Kale

SEASON: Cool or warm.
TRANSPLANT: Yes; grow for about four weeks before planting out, or direct-seed.
DAYS TO MATURITY: 50–65 days from direct-seeding.
COMMENTS: Kale is a must-grow vegetable; it's tender, tasty, nutritious,

and can be harvested in cool spring, hot summer, and even cold winter weather. Plants started in early spring become the size of small trees by fall, so they need to be set down the middle of a bed. For kale started later as only a late crop, plant two rows per bed with 12 inches between plants in a row.

Don't fault your composting system if kale stalks keep resurfacing to haunt you. They are very resistant to decay, so much so that the old stalks of one variety are fashioned into fancy walking sticks in Great Britain.

Kohlrabi

SEASON: Cool

TRANSPLANT: Yes, or direct-seed.

DAYS TO MATURITY: 35–45 days from direct-seeding.

COMMENTS: To me, kohlrabi tastes like a cabbage stalk (essentially, what it is); I don't like it or grow it. If you're a fan, plant four rows down a bed with 8 inches between plants in a row. If you really like it, the variety named 'Football' (a direct reference to its size) might especially appeal to you.

Leek

SEASON: Cool or warm.

TRANSPLANT: Yes; grow for 10 to 12 weeks before planting out, or direct-seed.

DAYS TO MATURITY: 75–115 days from direct-seeding.

COMMENTS: It takes a long season to grow big, fat leeks, so start seeds indoors in midwinter, then transplant seedlings to four rows per bed, spacing them 6 inches apart in the rows. No need for hilling up, as is traditionally recommended. Make a hole by pushing a ¾" diameter stick into the ground about 3" deep, drop in a leek seedling, then pour water into the hole to wash soil around the roots.

Given the price of leeks in supermarkets, growing them is one way to feel rich. (In Europe, however, they're sometimes called "poor man's asparagus.") Leeks are cold-hardy, which allows for harvesting almost all winter, especially if some fluffy mulch is thrown over them in fall to keep them and the soil from freezing.

Lettuce

SEASON: Cool.

TRANSPLANT: Yes; grow for about four weeks before planting out, or direct-seed.

DAYS TO MATURITY: 30–50 days; the earliest pickings are tender, baby leaves.

COMMENTS: I grow heading lettuces, such as Bibb and Romaine types, mostly as transplants spaced 10 inches apart in the row, often between crops such as beans or okra that fill in as the season progresses. For a solid bed of heading lettuce—a tapestry of colors and textures when varieties are combined—run three rows down a bed.

I grow leaf lettuces—and sometimes heading lettuces,

A tapestry of different lettuces: green leaf, red leaf, red tip, frilly leaf, butterhead, and Cos.

too—by just dropping seeds directly in furrows. I harvest by cutting leaves at ground level from a different portion of the row each time. The leaves grow back as I move on to another portion of the row for the next harvest. Alternately, young plants can be thinned out (and eaten) so the remaining plants grow larger.

Thinnings or individual heads of home-grown lettuce are absolutely delicious, each in their own way. The thinnings are very tender and mild. Individual heads are buttery or crunchy, with a more distinctive flavor bite.

Mâche

Season: Cool.
Transplant: No.
Days to Maturity: 50 days.
Comments: Mâche is delectable and unusually winter-hardy, which is not what you'd expect in such a delicately textured and flavored salad green. Sow seeds in cool weather, four rows per bed. I actually have better luck with self-sown seeds from plants that I let go to seed than I do from seeds I plant myself. This is not surprising when you consider that mâche is also called "corn salad" because it's a weed in European cornfields (in the Queen's English, corn is any grain *except* what we call "corn," which is "maize"). This easily checked "weed" is always welcome in my Weedless Gardening beds.

Melon

Season: Warm.
Transplant: Yes; grow for about four weeks before setting out; where seasons are long and warm, transplanting is unnecessary.
Days to Maturity: 75–120 days from planting seed.

COMMENTS: I haven't perfected spacing for melons yet. The plants grow fine but sprawl all over the place, even with hills of three plants, each spaced 3 feet apart down the middle of a bed. Low tomato cages have helped to add a vertical dimension, but even better would be a sturdy, temporary trellis along with deliberate pruning of the growing vines. When grown on trellises, support individual fruits in some sort of hammock.

Okra

SEASON: Warm.

TRANSPLANT: No.

DAYS TO MATURITY: 50–60 days.

COMMENTS: Plant two rows down each bed in warm soil, thinning the seedlings to a few inches apart. Where growing seasons are hot and long, okra plants will need more space, perhaps allowing only one row per bed, with that row flanked by other early, then late-season, cool-weather vegetables.

Onion

SEASON: Grows in cool and warm seasons, ripens in summer.

TRANSPLANT: Yes; grow for 10 to 12 weeks before planting out, direct-seed, or grow from "sets" (small bulbs).

DAYS TO MATURITY: 80–120 days from seeding (varieties that over-winter where winters are mild are planted in late summer for harvest the following year).

COMMENTS: Onions respond to spacing in terms of yield and size. To a point, the closer the spacing, the smaller the onions but the greater the total yield. For the medium- to large-size onions that I like, I plant five rows per bed, with 6 inches between plants in a row, or four rows per bed, with 4 inches between plants. (This spacing is for onions from sets or transplants, with varieties used for sets being easier to grow and storing better, and varieties used for transplants being sweeter and more tender.) Onions seeded directly in the garden do not grow as large, so they can be spaced closer.

You have greater choice in varieties if you grow onion transplants from seeds planted indoors. Northern gardeners grow long-day varieties, which bulb after plants have grown plenty of leaves. Southern gardeners grow short-day varieties; long-day types would never bulb there.

Parsley

SEASON: Cool or warm.

TRANSPLANT: Yes; grow for about six weeks before planting out, or direct-seed.

DAYS TO MATURITY: 75 days from sowing seed.

COMMENTS: Along with kale, parsley is another must-grow because it's easy to grow, yields for almost a year, is so nutritious, and tastes great. The seeds germinate slowly, but once they're finally up, they need only about 6 inches of space from one row to the next—that's five rows per bed. Or spot them in among other plants. You could also sow a row directly out into the garden. The seedlings will come up thickly, but they'll grow well and give you a parsley "hedge" to harvest from.

Parsnips

SEASON: Plant in spring for harvest in cool autumn or cold winter weather.

TRANSPLANT: No.

DAYS TO MATURITY: 120 days.

COMMENTS: I've grown parsnips every 15 years or so just to confirm my distaste for them. Parsnip is easy to grow and keeps well through winter, so if you like the taste, plant three rows per bed with plants spaced 4 inches apart in the row.

Don't rush the harvest on this vegetable. Cool weather brings out the sugars.

Peas

SEASON: Cool.

TRANSPLANT: No.

DAYS TO MATURITY: 50–65 days.

COMMENTS: Peas are another must-grow because they taste so good. The sugars in peas start changing to starch right after harvest, so you can never buy peas off a shelf that even come close in flavor to those you pick and eat right out of the garden.

Peas love cool weather so plant early, just as soon as the soil defrosts in spring (or forsythia starts to bloom). Where summers are cool, peas can also be grown as a late crop. Either way, plant a double row down the center of the bed, spacing the rows 4 inches apart with pea seeds dropped a couple of inches apart within each row. Trellis the peas and grow other crops flanking them in the bed.

My all-time favorites are the shelling types (specifically, the varieties 'Lincoln' and 'Green Arrow'), even if they do require some work to get at the peas. Among snap peas, which you eat pods and all after they fatten up, 'Sugar Snap' is excellent, although it demands a trellis at least 5 feet high. I grow it in a bed that borders a 5-foot fence. Snow peas, also called Chinese peas, should be picked when the developing peas just begin to swell in their flat pods.

Peppers

SEASON: Warm.

TRANSPLANT: Yes; grow for about 8 weeks before planting out.

DAYS TO MATURITY: 70–85 days to full, colorful ripeness.

COMMENTS: Set two rows of transplants down each bed, with plants 18 inches apart in the rows. Early greens such as lettuce, spinach, and/or arugula can fill the empty space between the rows as the peppers are filling in. I also have planted beets in that space, and they hold well there all summer, ready to be harvested as needed. I enjoy peppers only when they are fully ripe—red, yellow, purple, brown, or whatever color they eventually turn. Particularly good is the variety 'Sweet Italia,' also called 'Italian,' for its early harvest, reliability, and outstanding flavor.

Potatoes, Sweet

SEASON: Warm.

TRANSPLANT: Yes (from "slips," which are rooted stems).

DAYS TO MATURITY: Harvest in October (in the North, anytime before frost).

COMMENTS: Sweet potatoes, which love heat, are usually grown on mounds because of the warmer root environment created. Digging them surely disrupts the soil, but less so if the variety is a bunching type. The swollen roots of 'Bunch Porto Rico' and 'Vardaman' develop in tight clusters.

Potato, White

SEASON: Cool and warm.

TRANSPLANT: Yes; plant 2-ounce tubers or pieces of tubers.

DAYS TO MATURITY: 65–90 days.

Potato hills, showing old "seed" and new potatoes forming above them.

COMMENTS: The soil where white potatoes are grown is traditionally quite disrupted, first when the growing plants are hilled (that is, as the soil is drawn up against the stems), and second when they are dug for harvest. I set two rows of "seed" potatoes (small potatoes or pieces of potatoes for planting) down a bed a couple of inches deep, with 8 to 12 inches between them in the row. When the stems grow to about 6 inches tall, I hill soil up around them with a hoe. After that, I mulch the beds with grass clippings—but any other weed-free, fairly quick decomposing organic material would also do. Light turns tubers green and bitter, and this mulch keeps the developing tubers covered even as they grow or the mounds are pelted by rain.

Radish

SEASON: Cool.

TRANSPLANT: No.

DAYS TO MATURITY: 25–35 days for small radishes, 50–60 days for large ones.

COMMENTS: Small radishes grow quickly and take up little space. They like cool weather, so plant short rows here and there in spring and fall.

If you want a solid bed, plant five rows with only an inch or so between plants.

So-called winter radishes grow big, even to many pounds each. Choose varieties, length of time spent in the ground, and spacing according to how big a radish you want.

Rutabaga

SEASON: Plant in summer for harvest in cool autumn weather.

TRANSPLANT: No.

DAYS TO MATURITY: 90–100 days.

COMMENTS: Plant three rows down a bed, spacing plants 8 inches apart in the rows.

Salsify

SEASON: Plant in spring to grow all summer for harvest in cool autumn weather.

TRANSPLANT: No.

DAYS TO MATURITY: 120 days.

COMMENTS: Does this vegetable, also called vegetable oyster or oyster plant, really taste like oysters? No. Does it taste good? Yes. Plant this long-season root crop four rows per bed, with 6 inches between plants in the row.

Spinach

SEASON: Cool.

TRANSPLANT: No.

DAYS TO MATURITY: 35–45 days.

COMMENTS: Spinach matures quickly and loves cool weather, so squeeze rows in at the beginning and at the end of the season. For a solid bed, plant four rows, eventually thinning seedlings to 4 inches apart in the row.

Squash

SEASON: Warm.

TRANSPLANT: Not necessary, but sowing indoors one month early is useful for an extra-early crop of summer squash.

DAYS TO MATURITY: 45–55 days from seeding for summer squash; 90–105 days for winter squash.

COMMENTS: Summer squashes, such as zucchini, have a bushy growth habit and are monstrous plants, so put them in warm soil right down the middle of the beds. You could plant seeds every foot or so, but I find it easier to harvest if seeds are sown to give a couple of plants every 3 feet. So what if yield suffers a bit—the problem with zucchini is that there's usually too much of it.

Winter squashes are generally long-vining plants. They can be accommodated within beds if the vines are trained up a trellis, with seeds planted about 2 feet apart. I grow winter squash at the edge of the garden, where the vines can climb the fence or, if they like, ramble through the fence onto the adjoining field or lawn.

Swiss Chard

SEASON: Cool and warm.

TRANSPLANT: No.

DAYS TO MATURITY: 50–60 days.

COMMENTS: Swiss chard is easy to grow and nutritious, and it bears from spring right through summer and on into (in some cases, through) winter. I'm not a big fan of the taste, but if you like it, plant three or four rows per bed, spacing plants about 8 inches apart in the row. Keep picking the outer leaves as new ones develop in the center.

Tomato

SEASON: Warm.

TRANSPLANT: Yes, grow for about six weeks before planting out.

DAYS TO MATURITY: 50–80 days after transplanting.

COMMENTS: A sprawling tomato plant takes up a lot of space and bears a lot of fruit. A staked tomato plant takes up less space and yields cleaner and earlier fruit. Because staked plants can stand 18 inches apart and grow upward, they yield more from a given area of ground than sprawling plants. Only "indeterminate" varieties (noted on the seed packet) are suitable for staking, but these varieties, with higher leaf-to-fruit ratios, taste better anyway. You can plant two rows down a bed if you stake and ruthlessly prune the plants.

Restrict growth of closely spaced tomatoes to a single main stem per plant. Side shoots develop wherever a leaf joins the stem; just snap them off. Tie the main stem to the stake at least once a week.

Arrows indicate where side shoots are or have been snapped off to create a single-stemmed, staked tomato plant.

Choosing the right variety is the key to the most flavorful tomatoes. With cherry tomatoes, I concur with others who have tried 'Sungold'— it's the best, a beautiful persimmon orange and sweet-tart. Among my favorite full-size tomatoes are 'Belgian Giant,' 'Carmello,' 'Dona,' and 'Valencia.' 'San Marzano' and 'Amish Paste' cook up to delectable sauces. Sweet and juicy 'Anna Russian' is very good either fresh or cooked.

Turnip

Season: Plant in later summer for harvest in cool autumn weather.

Transplant: No.

Days to Maturity: 35–50 days.

Comments: A well-grown turnip might not compare with a tree-ripened peach, but it is a most flavorful vegetable, sweet and crisp. Good soil, adequate water, and timely planting are the secrets to tasty turnips. My late-summer plantings, which ripen in the cool days of autumn, taste the best. Plant four rows per bed, thinning plants to 6 inches apart in the row. The thinnings can be cooked for delicious turnip "greens."

CHAPTER SIX

Flower Gardens and Herbaceous Ground Covers

lower gardens and herbaceous ground covers take well to the methods of Weedless Gardening, and one option for avoiding soil compaction is tiptoeing through the tulips. But tiptoe very lightly. A step here and there near plants is tolerable because flower gardens and ground-cover plantings don't get the heavy traffic of vegetable gardens. Of course, you might steal in among the flower patch on occasion to snip some blossoms for a vase, to whiff a fragrant bouquet, to pull a few weeds, or to plant. Mostly, you'll just stand or sit outside the bed, or walk by it in admiration.

Plantings of flowers or ground covers encompass a broad spectrum of plants and garden styles, from formal Victorian-style bedding to informal mixed borders, wildflower meadows, and herbaceous ground covers. The layout of each of these gardens is obviously going to vary; likewise the ground treatment. Tilling is still not an option, and would be near impossible for any area with a fair share of perennial plants.

The need for watering also varies with the kind of planting as well as growing conditions. A flower bed of native or exotic plants adapted to local conditions, or a wildflower meadow with plants chosen for their adaptability, should need little or no supplemental watering. The same holds true for ground-cover plants well matched to their site. For the initial and occasional subsequent (if that) watering needed by these plantings, just drag out the traditional sprinkler.

Flower gardens requiring higher culture demand a regular supply of water for peak performance. Peak performance is the key phrase here. Many flower gardens get along fine with little or no watering, but where peak performance is wanted—especially where plants and climate are not optimally matched—watering is easiest and most efficiently done with drip irrigation. Formal beds of annuals and some perennial mixed borders are prime candidates for drip irrigation

Dripperlines can be snaked within beds sufficiently close so wetting fronts overlap between adjacent lines. Where high humidity in addition to soil moisture is needed, half-inch headers can be run into beds, with micro-sprinklers on short stakes plugged into them at intervals close enough so the spray patterns overlap.

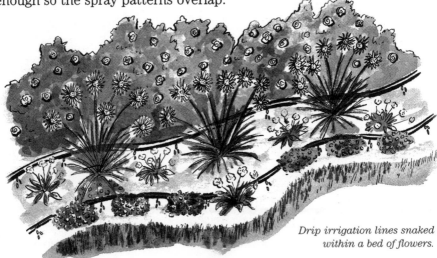

Drip irrigation lines snaked within a bed of flowers.

Formal Bedding

The segue from vegetable gardens to formal bedding in Weedless Gardening is a natural one. Like most vegetables, traditional bedding plants are annuals—in this case, annual flowers laid out in colorful patterns in beds. What bedding plants lack in permanence they offer in nonstop color from one end of the season to the other. This nonstop color demands relatively good fertility, but generally not as much as is necessary for vegetables. Beds are needed for the sake of style and for the health of the plants and soil; after all, annuals must be planted and cleaned up every year without trampling the soil.

A primary consideration is the layout and size of flower beds. Bed layout contributes to

Grass, if non-invasive, makes attractive and utilitarian paths in formal flower beds.

the design of the overall garden, whether it is the outline of a large, single bed or a pattern of smaller beds.

Ideally, you should be able to reach anywhere in a bed with your feet firmly planted on an adjacent path or lawn. Minimum width for a path is 18 inches, and wider paths provide inducement for more leisurely strolling among the flowers. Any of the coverings for paths mentioned in previous chapters are suitable, but lawn grass is particularly well matched with the tenor of this garden. Be prepared to maintain lawn-grass edges crisply and in high fashion by going around the garden, as needed, with your half-moon edger.

Maximum width for a bed that can be reached from either side is

Flagstone stepping-stones carry the visitor into this flower garden.

Bricks laid in square pads provide firm footing and prevent soil compaction in the garden.

about 48 inches. (The width is greater than the maximum for vegetable beds because not as much reaching goes on into a flower bed.) If you absolutely must have wider beds, there are options beyond tramping on the soil. One way to avoid compaction is to work from a plank that you lay on the bed to distribute your weight. The other option is to

Coral stepping-stones lend a tropical air to this flower garden.

place stepping-stones strategically and permanently in the beds. Like the shapes of the paths and beds themselves, stepping-stones should figure into the design of the garden. Consider their shapes, locations, and materials—for example, flagstone for a New England look, flat pieces cut from coral for a Florida look, bricks laid in squared pads for a Virginia look.

Maintenance of formal bedding gardens is no different from that of vegetable gardens. Plant and then clean up at the end of the season with minimum disturbance of the soil, keep the edges neat, and weed as needed. Rather than leaving the beds bare through winter, as is usually done, consider planting a late-season cover crop to protect and improve the soil, and to avoid the bleakness of bare ground. An annual dressing of an inch (or more) of compost will do its part in weeding and feeding the beds. Other tidy mulch possibilities include buckwheat, rice, or oat hulls. Additional fertilizer is unnecessary with an annual compost mulch, and is unlikely to be needed even with other mulches except in poor soils. If a little boost is needed, sprinkle soybean meal (at 2 pounds or less per 100 square feet) or some other high-nitrogen fertilizer over plant beds before mulching. Avoid the temptation to overfertilize with nitrogen, for it can lead to excess leafy growth at the expense of flowers.

Wildflower Meadows and Ground Covers

Wildflower meadows and ground covers represent the other end of the flower garden spectrum from formal bedding. In meadows and ground covers, we won't find planted beds that are seasonally bare, and rarely are paths even defined. With wildflower meadows and ground covers, total year-round plant coverage is the goal.

Wildflower meadows and ground covers are not the kinds of decorative plantings often frequented up close, so there's no real need for beds and paths anyway. These plantings look as good from afar as they do close-up, and the perennials or self-sowing biennials and

A path into a meadow is created and maintained with a mower.

annual plants have little need to be fiddled with. Occasional trodding upon the ground, especially when it is dense with vegetation and not wet, should do no harm. If traffic is frequent, paths should be laid out through a ground cover or, in the case of a meadow, cut through in swaths.

Readying the Ground

Despite the low maintenance demanded by a mature meadow or ground-cover planting, thorough preparation and planning are needed to establish them—especially meadows. Don't let the ubiquitous "meadows in a can" (containers of meadow plant seeds) or some other promise of an instant meadow fool you into believing that just sprinkling seeds or rolling out a seeded, biodegradable carpet on top of the ground will result in a carefree riot of season-long color. Thorough preparation is also needed because meadow plants are not set out in neat rows easily weeded by hand or by hoe. Neat rows, after all, would ruin the random charm of a meadow. Ground-cover plants, in contrast, can and should be blocked off or set in rows because they eventually fill in to form a solid mass of a single type of plant. In either case, though, the goal is to create conditions as weed-free as possible *before* setting out plants or sowing seeds.

The first consideration is the scale of the planting because preparations for a small site differ from those for a large site. Small sites need only mowing (and perhaps fertilizing), smothering with wetted paper, and covering. The ideal covering for the paper is something weed-free and not too rich, and if seeds are to be planted, something in which they can sprout and grow.

Ground-cover plants, wildflower transplants, or grass transplants can be planted right into wood chips that are not too coarse. (Meadows do need a certain amount of grasses—preferably, bunch grasses—for soil stabilization.) If the chips were sitting around wet and were already on their way to decomposition, all the better. Wood chips are widely available and often free, but other weed-free organic materials such as marsh hay, sawdust, and straw are also suitable. Compost might be too rich for such plantings, and could promote the growth of aggressive interlopers—weeds, that is—over plants that thrive in leaner soil.

If you're going to plant a small area by sowing seeds rather than setting out transplants, cover the wetted paper with a thin layer (an inch or so) of compost. Even better, dilute the compost by thoroughly mixing it with equal parts of some weed-free sandy soil, even pure sand, before spreading it. This mix creates a nice seedbed and dilutes nutrients in the compost.

The large meadow presents a different challenge: a great deal of ground, more than can be feasibly covered with paper and compost or a special mix of compost and sand. Successfully planting a large meadow is a combination of art and science because each site presents its own special wrinkles. To be able to capitalize on each year's learning, consider preparing the ground and planting a large meadow by portions each year. A good start in any case is to begin by mowing—literally, to even out the playing field.

Once mowed, the vegetation needs to be killed, and either spraying with an herbicide or tilling the soil is the most practical way to do this on a large scale. Although *herbicide* and *tillage* would be curse words elsewhere in this book, their judicious, one-time use might be justified in this case. The herbicide usually recommended would be glyphosate (such as Roundup), sprayed just after plants that were mowed begin actively growing again. The toxin is drawn into the leaves, then kills all parts of the plants. Glyphosate is a nonselective herbicide, so take precautions: Keep the spray nozzle low, adjusting it for larger droplet sizes to avoid drift and injury to nontarget areas, and spray when the weather is calm. By following usage instructions to the letter, plants should be visibly dead within two weeks and nontarget plants should remain unharmed. No need to wait until plants show that they are dead before planting. Seeds can be sown or transplants set out—with, of course, minimal soil disturbance—as soon as the spray has dried. Be aware that controversy surrounds the safety of glyphosate; readers should research this issue before using it, or else consider other options in ground preparation.

Tillage certainly presents a more bucolic scene for ground preparation than herbicide spraying. Repeated passes with a rototiller, at two-week intervals, are needed to thoroughly break up and kill plants. Tillage should be shallow in order to minimize the amount of soil (and hence, weed seeds) brought to the surface, and to minimize the destruction of soil structure and organic matter. To fight off weeds that will assuredly sprout, and to protect the surface from wind and water erosion, sow a cover crop immediately after the last (second or third) tillage. Sequential sowings of cover crops, with each crop's growth following the death by age, cold, mowing, or undercutting of the previous one, gives better weed control than just a single cover-crop planting.

Seeds of each successive cover crop could be scattered into a living stand of the previous cover crop toward the end of the latter crop's tenure. These seeds will germinate and grow as the existing stand dies away and flops to the ground. The optimum cover-crop plants, or their sequence, will vary according to climate and soil conditions. (See Selected Cover Crops on pages 50–51 for possibilities.)

Planting

Timing is critical for getting the actual meadow or ground-cover plants off to a good start ahead of weeds—especially when your attention is spread over areas measured in acres or in thousands of square feet. Generally, the best time for planting is just before the season of greatest natural rainfall (autumn in the western United States, for example) or when soil will be consistently moist because of a combination of rainfall and cool temperatures (autumn and spring in the eastern United States). Autumn planting has its benefits even with seeds that won't sprout until spring. The combination of rain and snow, and the ground's freezing and thawing in winter, opens up tiny cracks in the soil that snug seeds against it by spring. Some seeds even *need* to be exposed to a period of cool weather followed by warm weather (signaling for them that winter is over) before they will sprout. Timing for natural rainfall is not as critical for smaller areas that can be hand-watered.

Fine-tune your planting according to the kinds of plants you're growing. Transplants used for ground covers or small meadows must

OPTIMUM TIME FOR PLANTING MEADOW OR GROUND COVER

PLANT MATERIAL	COLD-WINTER AREAS	MILD-WINTER AREAS
Transplants	Early spring, late summer	Autumn
Seeds of cool-weather plants	Late autumn	Early autumn
Seeds of warm-weather plants	Late spring	Late spring

take firm hold of the soil before winter in areas where frost penetrates the soil. Therefore, in cold-winter locales, set transplants in the ground either in early spring or in late summer, with the latter timing allowing for at least six weeks of growth before cold weather. Sow seeds in early fall where winters do not get cold enough to kill young seedlings. Where winters are frigid, either sow seeds in late fall, after temperatures have turned too cold for germination, or wait until spring.

The optimum time to sow seeds that germinate only in warm weather—these include some grasses and annual flowers such as Cape daisy, annual phlox, and prairie aster—is late spring. Or take your chances and sow these warmth-lovers in late fall or early spring, and count on their being in place and ready to grow when temperatures finally warm.

A mixed handful of large and small, winged, fuzzy, and smooth seeds is not easy to spread evenly over an area of ground intended for a meadow. For even distribution, first mix the seeds with some inert material such as sand. Then divide the

Spreading meadow seeds in two different directions ensures more even distribution.

mix into two equal batches that you sow separately, the second batch spread in a direction perpendicular to the first.

Keep ground disturbance to a minimum after sowing seeds. Planting in standing vegetation that is slated to flop down dead before meadow seeds sprout entails no further preparation. But after planting in compost or the compost-plus-sand mix, rake the seed lightly into the surface, roll it with a lawn roller, or cover it with a thin layer of some weed-free mulch such as straw or salt-marsh hay.

Maintenance

Begin maintenance of a meadow or ground cover almost as soon as it's planted. If you used transplants, and natural rainfall isn't cooperative, you must water them. Keep any weeds that appear in check by hand-pulling or (possible only with regularly laid out ground-cover plants) with shallow hoeing.

Good soil preparation and timely planting do their share to help avoid weed problems; still, you should always have an eye out for weeds. As with weeding a garden, short but regular forays through your meadow or ground cover are the easiest and most effective way to keep the area weed-free. Long periods of neglect necessitate massive makeovers.

Cut, pull, and dig to remove weeds, whichever seems most appropriate for the weed at hand. Cutting is sometimes effective here because it checks weed growth just long enough for the weed to be smothered by the mass of surrounding greenery.

Occasional attention to weeds is pretty much the only regular maintenance needed by ground covers. Yes, the planting may need supplemental water in an unusually dry season. And a planting that seems to

Periodic mowing, at left, or burning, at right, keeps a meadow refreshed.

be sulking for no apparent reason might be perked up by nothing more than an autumn topdressing of shredded leaves, compost, or some other fine organic material. In all likelihood, neither watering nor topdressing will be needed.

A meadow needs more to keep it going than a ground-cover planting; it is a dynamic community of plants that, left alone, changes over time. In the Northeast, for example, an untended meadow usually becomes a forest. The way to slow or prevent change is, initially, to choose plants that will be sublimely happy with site conditions, and after that, to periodically mow or burn over the whole planting. Mowing or burning lets sunshine reach low-growing plants and keeps woody plants from invading and eventually converting the meadow to forest.

For centuries, fire has been part of the growth cycle of prairies, and its use can spill over to meadows, with their abundance of wildflowers rather than grasses. The season for burning is spring, before warm weather has spurred plant growth and while the soil is still wet, on a day with barely a whisper of a breeze. Precautions include creating nonflammable firebreaks (bare soil, mown lawn, etc.) to halt the spread of the fire beyond desired areas, clearing away nearby flammable materials, having a knowledgeable crew ready and emergency water on hand. It might also be necessary to obtain permission from local agencies before you can burn.

Mowing a meadow is less exciting than burning one, but is also effective. Once a year is needed, with late summer or fall being the usual season for the job. Late mowing helps disperse some seeds and sends the meadow into winter looking trim. Mowing instead in early spring leaves the meadow more interesting to look at through winter, with seed heads and stalks poking up. If your meadow also provides herbage for mulch and compost, mow as frequently as needed.

In Praise Of the Scythe

At first blush, the scythe may seem to be an archaic mowing tool, but consider the benefits. I can mow about 500 square feet in 15 minutes. A gasoline mower might do that job in a fraction of the time, but consider the money spent to buy the mower and the time and money spent maintaining, repairing, and keeping it fed with gasoline and oil. My scythe causes no air pollution and requires about 10 seconds of maintenance with a whetstone every half hour or so.

Mowing with a scythe offers greater time flexibility than power mowing. I don't worry about grass and weeds growing too long to mow because my scythe blade cuts as easily through 3-foot-high growth as it does through 3-inch-high growth.

Austrian-style scythe.

The tool is also quiet, so I don't have to schedule my mowing for a neighborly hour—even 5:30 in the morning won't bother anyone. My neighbor has gotten completely bogged down in her tractor at a wet spot that adjoins our property; with my scythe and a pair of waterproof boots, I can do my work anywhere.

The scythe also brings psychological and physical benefits. Tennyson wrote of the "sound to rout the brood of cares, the sweep of scythe in morning dew." Despite its repetitive motion, scything is an art that demands active participation, a ready awareness to "read the land" so the swing can be modified as necessary to suit the terrain and plants. In Tolstoy's *Anna Karenina*, Levin "felt the scythe become "a body full of life and consciousness of its own, and as though by magic, without thinking of it, the work turned out regular and well-finished of itself. These were [his] most blissful moments."

With regard to the purely physical benefits, consider the words of social scientist and homesteader Scott Nearing, who died at the age of 100: "I started scything in my teens, and have cut grass and hay with the same swing for more than 80 years. It is a first-class fresh-air exercise that stirs the blood and flexes the muscles while it clears the meadows."

To make scything truly enjoyable and efficient, just any old scythe will not do. The best is the Austrian-style scythe, distinguished by its lightweight blade hammered razor-sharp.

Sources for Austrian Scythes

- Lee Valley Tools
12 East River Street
Ogdensburg, NY 13669
800-871-8158
www.leevalley.com

- A. M. Leonard
P.O. Box 816
Piqua, OH 45356
800-543-8955
www.amleo.com

- The Marugg Co.
P.O. Box 1418
Tracy City, TN 37387
931-592-5042

A push mower is not the machine for mowing a meadow; it mows too close to the ground and cuts through tall vegetation with difficulty, if at all. A sit-down tractor or a walk-behind tractor with a rotary blade or sickle bar (much like electric hedge shears) makes the quickest work of a meadow. The advantage of the rotary mower is that it mows *and* chops the vegetation. If the cut herbage lays so thickly on top of the ground after mowing that it will smother plants, go over the area again with the rotary mower or rake it up. For a smaller area (or smaller investment), a weed whacker is sometimes recommended, but my mowing tool of choice—for low maintenance, flexibility, and sheer joy of use—is a scythe.

In spite of weeding and burning or mowing, don't expect your meadow to eventually settle into a steady state where it is the same year after year. You can stave off change, but it will come with year-to-year vagaries of local weather, aging of plants, your mowing habits (frequency, height, and season), and what mix of plants you started with. The smaller the area and better the plants are adapted to the site, the more easily you can maintain the status quo. But then again, change through the seasons and over the years is part of the beauty and interest of a meadow—as long as the site remains a meadow.

The Mixed Flower Border

Straddle the fence between formal bedding and a wildflower meadow or ground-cover planting, and what you find is another style of flower garden—the mixed flower border. It is the kind of flower planting most of us are likely to have, even if we also plant flowers on either side of that figurative fence. In the mixed flower border, we find annual, biennial, and perennial flowers happily coexisting with each other and even with shrubs and small trees. Aesthetically, this garden has almost everything: woody plants defining space and providing a verdant backdrop and seasonal color; months of nonstop color from annual flowers; and seasonal color highlights from perennial and biennial flowers. One plant we don't want in this mixed garden is, of course, weeds.

The same principles apply to keeping the mixed flower border healthy, happy, and weed-free as apply to any other plot of ground in the weedless garden. To wit, minimize disruption of the soil layers, avoid soil compaction and bare soil, and weed regularly. Apply the first principles, and the last—regular weeding—requires only a few pleasant minutes a week.

Well-defined paths and planted areas may (or may not) figure into your mixed border's design. Here the plants and soil require little regular attention. Mostly, you'll enter this garden for pleasure and won't have to reach every area with your feet planted on a fixed walkway. You can designate walkways among your plants with stepping-stones of flagstone or short rounds of wood, or by always walking in the same places. Or identify areas for walking with a mulch that looks different from that used in planted areas.

Aesthetics might dictate just what mulch you decide to use around plants. I use autumn leaves in my blowsy beds. Where something neater that stays put is desired, use pine needles, wood chips, grass clippings, sawdust, or hulls of oats, rice, or cottonseed. Some gardeners insist on seeing soil around their plants, but will settle for what looks like soil. If you are of this ilk, cover the ground with a chocolate-brown blanket of buckwheat or cocoa bean hulls; the latter gives a chocolatey aroma as well. Peat is another weed-free organic material that looks like soil but doesn't make a particularly good mulch. It provides little nutrition, and once it dries sitting on top of the ground, it's hard to wet again. Rainfall beads up and runs off dry peat just like it does off a newly waxed car.

Be careful when mulching young seedlings, succulents, and some alpine plants. Piling mulch up against thin, young stems causes them to rot, so leave a little breathing space between young seedlings' stems

Mulch protects the ground in this mixed border, keeps plants happy, and suppresses weeds.

Sources for Flower Seeds and Ground-Cover Plants

• Bluestone Perennials, 7211 Middle Ridge Road, Madison, OH 44057, 800-852-5243, www.bluestoneperennials.com

• W. Atlee Burpee & Co., 300 Park Avenue, Warminster, PA 18974, 800-888-1447, www.burpee.gardens.com

• Harris Seeds, P.O. Box 24966, Rochester, NY 14624, 800-514-4441, www.harrisseeds.com

• Milaeger's Gardens, 4838 Douglas Avenue, Racine, WI 53402, 800-669-9956, www.milaegersgardens.com

• Park Seed Co., 1 Parkton Avenue, Greenwood, SC 29647, 800-845-3369, www.parkseed.com

• Plants of the Southwest, Route 6, Box 11A, Agua Fria, Sante Fe, NM 87501, 505-471-2212, www.plantsofthesouthwest.com

• Prairie Nursery, P.O. Box 306, Westfield, WI 53964, 800-476-9453, www.prairienursery.com

• Tripple Brook Farm, 37 Middle Road, Southampton, MA 01073, 413-527-4626, www.tripplebrookfarm.com

• Wayside Gardens, 1 Garden Lane, Hodges, SC 29695, 800-845-1124, www.waysidegardens.com

and the mulch. Succulents and alpine plants like a lean soil that tends to be dry, so mulch with a thin layer of some nonabsorbent material such as seed hulls (rice, buckwheat, cocoa bean, etc.), sand, or gravel.

Notice that I did not mention using compost as a mulch for flowering plants in the mixed border; the reason is that compost could make the soil too rich. True, some flowers do demand a rich soil; scattering a few shovelfuls of compost around plants like anemone, astilbe, delphinium, goat's beard, hostas, and monkshood will satisfy their appetites. But many other flowering plants channel any extra fertility

Dividing Perennials

With age, some perennial flowers form clumps that die out in the center as new growth spreads at the edges. Crowns of other perennials inch upward out of the ground each year, their centers eventually dying from exposure to the elements. The result, in either case, is fewer flowers. When this happens, dig up and divide the clump.

Soil disruption is inevitable when a perennial is divided. Typically, division is done in spring as young leaves emerge. The idea is to save and replant the youngest and most exuberant parts.

No need to turn the soil over and over, though. Just work a shovel or spading fork into the ground around the edge of the clump, pushing up and down on the handle to lever the clump up and shake dirt loose from the roots. Eventually, the clump will be sitting almost on top of the ground.

Back-to-back garden forks divide a perennial clump.

Take apart the clump with a sharp spade, a large knife, pruning shears, or your bare hands—whatever it takes—teasing off healthy pieces of young growth, usually found toward the outer edge of the clump. Then replant, mulching the soil with compost or some other organic material after planting, and finally, water the plant in.

Perennial flowers vary in their need for division. To look their best, perennials like asters or hardy chrysanthemums need to be dug up, cut apart, and re-

into making leaves rather than flowers.

Spread mulch of any sort around plants in the mixed flower border at any time of year. I find that autumn is the most convenient time, and mulch applied then also protects plants from winter cold and from being heaved out of the ground as it freezes and thaws. In autumn, mulches can be spread over the whole bed, right on top of

planted every spring. Invasive perennials such as
bee balm, tansy, goldenrod, and artemisia do
not need frequent division to spruce them up,
but rather to keep them from wandering beyond their allotted space.

Other perennials can go a longer stretch
without division. Armeria, phlox, coral
bells, Canterbury bells, cerastium, Siberian
and Japanese irises, veronica, yarrow, and

*Save young, vigorous pieces
for replanting.*

Shasta daisies need division only every three or four years. And 10 years might
elapse before a spade or fork must be put to a bed of lady's mantle, hosta,
echinops, daylily, Solomon's seal, or candytuft.

A few perennials don't want to be divided
in spring. Oriental poppies, bleeding hearts,
bearded irises, Virginia cowslips, and other
perennials that go dormant in midsummer
should be dug up and divided at that time.
And think twice before dividing helle-
bores, peonies, monkshood, butterfly
weeds, lupines, and baby's breath at all.
These flowers need division perhaps once a
decade, if that. Initially, they resent the
treatment and show it by not blooming
again for a year or more.

*Replant young pieces, giving each
adequate space in which to grow.*

most plants after their leaves die down. Perennials that retain green
leaves through winter, however, should not be covered at all where
winters are mild. Where winters are cold, wait to cover such plants
until the soil has frozen about an inch deep. Come spring, peek
beneath the mulch and push it aside as soon as you see new yellow
(because of lack of light) leaves unfurling.

Planting Bulbs

Bulbs are among the easiest plants to put in the soil without disrupting it. Use a bulb planter (a cylindrical metal tool that you push into the ground to withdraw a cylinder of soil), drop the bulb into the waiting hole, then plop the cylinder of soil back on top of it. If the soil isn't crumbly, ensure good bulb-to-soil contact by first loosening up the soil in the bottom of the hole.

You might not be able to push the bulb planter into every type of soil, especially one that's too stony. If that's the case use a trowel, thrusting it straight into the ground if possible, then pulling it toward you to open up a hole. If you must scoop out the soil, do so, but replace it with minimum mixing.

Sometimes bulbs have to be taken out of the soil. Dig up tender bulbs for winter storage or hardy bulbs for dividing the way you dig up weeds with stout roots, except even more carefully so you don't damage them. Thrust a trowel, long-bladed spade, or garden fork into the ground near the bulb, then lever up on it as you tug up on the foliage. Tug gently because the foliage on dormant or nearly dormant bulbs is getting ready to detach.

Some perennials don't want their crowns covered with mulch—ever! Such plants include coral bells, delphiniums, irises, violas, oriental poppies, and sedums. If you use a loose mulch like autumn leaves in your bed, keep winter winds from blowing the leaves over the crowns of these particular plants. A bushel basket inverted over each plant is the traditional way to do this, but a foot-high cylinder of wire fencing also does the trick. Even prettier is a foot-high tepee of bamboo stakes.

CHAPTER SEVEN

Trees, Shrubs, and Vines, Including Fruit Plants

he ending to Joyce Kilmer's ode to trees, "only God can make a tree," may be true enough (as was Woody Allen's addendum that the hardest part was sticking the bark on). But for best growth once a tree or shrub or vine is made, it's up to us mortals to step in to snuggle the plant into its new surroundings and give it some care thereafter.

Weeds are not often a problem with established trees, shrubs, and vines. A lawnmower does all the "weeding" when these plants are grown with lawn right up to their trunks and stems. And incorporating a woody plant into, say, a mixed border or ground-cover planting brings no special weed problems to the planting. Still, applying the techniques of Weedless Gardening to trees, shrubs, and vines gets them off to a better start and keeps them happier as they age, even if weed control is only an incidental benefit.

Planting a Tree, Vine, or Shrub

Plant a tree, shrub, or vine without digging? Not likely. Then again, nestling a woody plant into its new home has gotten a lot easier in recent years—not from new technology in digging equipment, but from research into planting techniques and plant responses. The old saying that it's better to plant a $5 tree in a $50 hole than a $50 tree in a $5 hole has been put to rest. Modern wisdom is good for both the plant and your back.

Location, Location

Before you reach for your shovel, take a moment—or a day, a week, a month—to think about the match between your plant and its proposed location. Trees, vines, and shrubs are permanent features in the landscape, which makes site selection and matching the plant to its environment especially important.

Trees, shrubs, and vines have wide-spreading roots. Even if a bathtub-size hole could be filled with soil tailored exactly to a sapling's needs, in time the roots would venture out into surrounding native ground. Tree roots normally spread half again to three times the radius of their branches.

With site conditions defined, put together a list of compatible plants and then choose from this group. This scenario is a lot more fun than starting with a plant, perhaps an impulse purchase spurred on by a glorious spring day, then pushing it around in a wheelbarrow, trying to figure out where it might look and grow best.

The irrationality brought on by glorious spring days is one of many reasons that fall is generally a better time than spring for planting trees, shrubs, and vines. The soil is warm and not overly wet in fall, making it mellower for digging. And there's less rush to get a plant into the ground because stems and leaves won't start growing until spring. Root growth generally begins before shoot growth in spring, so fall-planted trees, shrubs, and vines are already in place and ready to grow as soon as winter cold makes its final exit.

A few plants do not take well to bare-root fall planting. Included among them are those with fleshy roots such as magnolia, yellowwood, and dogwood, as well as hickory, beech, sweet gum, and tupelo. (See the chart on the following page for a more extensive list.) Aside from these exceptions, consider planting trees, shrubs, and vines in fall—and enjoy the extra time you have in spring.

Ready the Hole

New research shows that tree roots establish most quickly in a planting hole only two to three times the diameter of the root ball and no deeper than necessary for the plant to stand at the same level as it did in the nursery (or higher, if a mound is needed for improved drainage). A plant needs a firm base of undisturbed soil that won't settle with time.

Figure out the width of your proposed hole, then strip the sod or weeds from that area. Do

Stripping sod at the tree hole.

TREES BEST TRANSPLANTED, WHEN BARE-ROOT, IN SPRING

SCIENTIFIC NAME	COMMON NAME
Abies spp.	Fir
Betula spp.	Birch
Carpinus caroliniana	American hornbeam
Carya spp.	Hickory, pecan
Cladrastis lutea	American yellowwood
Cornus florida	Flowering dogwood
Diospyros virginiana	Common persimmon
Fagus spp.	Beech
Ginkgo biloba	Ginkgo
Ilex opaca	American holly
Juglans spp.	Walnut, butternut
Koelreuteria paniculata	Golden rain tree
Laburnum spp.	Laburnum
Larix spp.	Larch
Liquidambar styraciflua	Sweet gum
Liriodendron tulipifera	Tulip tree, yellow poplar
Magnolia spp.	Magnolia
Nyssa sylvatica	Tupelo, black gum, sour gum
Ostrya virginiana	American hop hornbeam
Oxydendrum arboreum	Sourwood
Populus spp.	Poplar
Prunus spp.	Cherry, plum
Pseudolarix amabilis	Golden larch
Quercus spp.	Oak
Salix spp.	Willow
Sassafras albidum	Sassafras
Taxodium spp.	Cypress
Tsuga spp.	Hemlock

this by first cutting straight down through the surface vegetation around the edge of your proposed hole with a shovel or grass edger. Then work a flat-bladed shovel or sod stripper just beneath the vegetation to lift it off. Add this material to your compost pile.

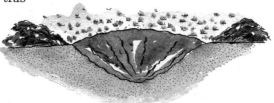

Make the planting hole cone-shaped and more broad than deep.

Rather than digging full depth right out to the edge of your planting hole, taper the depth from ground level at the edges to full depth at the center, in a cone shape. This opens the way for the bulk of new roots, most of which grow horizontally near the surface. When you finish, rough up the inside of the hole so roots can more easily penetrate the surrounding soil.

The only justification for more vigorous hole digging is when plant and soil are not well matched—if, for example, the soil is very deficient in phosphorus, or if lime or sulfur is needed to alter the acidity. These materials move very slowly down into the soil. But there's still no need to be overzealous with your digging. Dig amendments into only enough ground to nourish the roots for a year or so. Beyond where roots will spread in a year, soil additives can later be sprinkled on top of the ground to gradually work into the soil.

When I've planted blueberries, which thrive best in soils that are very rich in organic matter and very acidic, I've mixed acidic peat moss right into the soil of the

Lime or sulfur spread on top of the ground beyond the planting hole will work its way into the soil by the time roots spread.

planting hole. Peat decomposes very slowly, and slight settling is not detrimental to a shrub, which is always replacing old stems with new ones originating from below ground. (Trees, in contrast, don't like their one or few permanent trunks buried.) Beyond the hole, an annual mulch of a few inches of sawdust gradually rots to enrich the soil where the roots eventually spread. Sprinkling sulfur on the ground every few years maintains soil acidity.

Never mix fertilizer into a planting hole. Fertilizer placed there could burn new roots, and soil nutrients play a minor role, if any, in the growth of trees, shrubs, or vines the first year that they are transplanted to a new site.

Ready the Plant

Your role in starting any woody plant on a long and healthy life begins as soon as you have it in hand. Until planting, keep the roots moist and (if the plant was bare-root or balled-and-burlapped) cool. Plump up the roots of bare-root plants by soaking them in a bucket of water for about eight hours. Small plants can be kept cool in a refrigerator, with their roots in plastic wrap. Larger plants will keep cool and moist on the north side of your house or garage, with their roots temporarily nestled in just enough moist soil to cover them.

Just before planting, take your last look at the roots of your tree, shrub, or vine. If the plant is bare-root, use sharp pruning shears to cut back (to healthy tissue) any roots damaged or blackened by disease. Also shorten any odd roots that are too lanky to fit conveniently into the planting hole. Even as you take the plant out to its planting hole, keep the roots moist in a bucket of water or with a cover of wet burlap.

If your plant is in a pot, slide it out. Untangle and splay out any

Planting Myths

Excavation of a bathtub-size planting hole is not the only planting tradition that turns out not to be best for woody plants. The suggestion to throw gravel or some other coarse material into the bottom of a planting hole (a deep hole, of course) where soil drainage needs improvement is another misguided, dated idea. The thought was that gravel or loose material would help drain away water. What really happens is just the opposite: A so-called perched water table forms above the layer of gravel and does not drain until the upper layer becomes saturated. (You can observe this if you saturate a sponge with water and then hold it in the air without squeezing it. Does the water drop into the equivalent of a very large pore space below? No.)

Another item often recommended for the bottom of a planting hole was the sod that was cut out from the lawn when the hole was dug. This organic material again was counted on to improve water drainage and enrich the soil deep down near the roots. In truth, drainage is adversely affected for the same reason that a gravel layer impedes drainage. As for enriching the soil near the roots, the bulk of all plants' feeder roots lie near the soil surface, not deep within the soil. And as the sod slowly decomposes, probably putrefying from lack of oxygen, the soil—and the plant—sinks.

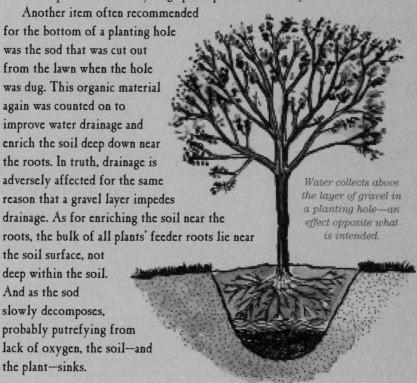

Water collects above the layer of gravel in a planting hole—an effect opposite what is intended.

roots that tried to outgrow the container and were forced to circle around inside. Also shorten any that are overly lanky. If the roots are too tightly bound together to untangle, cut four slits, each an inch deep, from top to bottom into the outside of the root ball with a sharp knife. Once you have large roots loosened, use a stick to tease outward some of the smaller roots from the outside of the root ball. If your plant is balled-and-burlapped, do nothing more than avoid breaking the root ball, along with its clinging roots.

Settle the Plant in Place

The effect of a good or bad planting technique can resonate for decades. If the plant is bare-root, set it atop a mound of soil that you've replaced in the hole. A convenient way to move a balled-and-burlapped

---

What Goes Around Comes Around

In 1919 the Duke of Bedford and Spencer Pickering published *Science and Fruit Growing*, the results of their studies at the Woburn Experimental Fruit Farm. Much of what they discovered debunked prevalent horticultural advice of the day—and today. Of topical interest was their study comparing trees that were "roughly planted" with those that were "carefully planted." Roots of roughly planted trees were "not trimmed, they were huddled into small holes, and then rammed into the ground."

The findings: Growth suffered somewhat the year of planting, but thereafter roughly planted trees and shrubs of many different kinds of fruits grew notably better than their carefully planted counterparts. Benefit was attributed to the intimate soil-root contact that resulted when the wet soil was rammed against the roots. The small planting hole, which forced roots to quickly grow out into the surrounding undisturbed soil, was also considered a benefit.

plant is by putting it on a tarp and pulling the tarp. Once the plant is in the hole, cut loose the strings binding the burlap and tuck one side of the burlap and tarp as close to the base of the plant as possible. Slightly rocking the plant—and a few more cuts into the burlap, if necessary—should allow you to remove the burlap and tarp with minimal disturbance to the root ball. Always remove the burlap because some types do not decompose in the soil; left in place, the material can strangle a plant.

Whether your plant started out bare-root, potted, or balled-and-burlapped, backfill soil from the planting hole once it's in place. As you backfill, use a stick or your fingers to work the soil up against and among the roots; if they're exposed to any large air spaces remaining in the soil, they'll dry out. Periodically check the planting depth as you fill, by laying a straight board across the planting hole and making adjustments as necessary. The change in color of the bark tells you how deeply the stem of a bare-root plant stood in the nursery. Finally, firm the soil up to ground level.

If surface water will flow away from the plant because you've planted on a mound or on sloping ground, build up a berm of soil a few inches high in a ring slightly wider than the spread of the roots. Left in place for a season or two, this miniature dike will corral rain or waterings until enough roots venture beyond into new ground.

Next, spread a 3-inch depth of wood chips or straw mulch over the bare ground. Don't pile mulch directly against a tree trunk or it may cause rotting. Mulch modulates soil temperatures, keeping roots of fall-planted trees, shrubs, and vines growing long into the fall. It also prevents heaving of plants in winter, and keeps roots cool and moist in summer—whether the plants were set in ground in spring or fall. Any mulch spread beyond the planting hole can be placed on top of paper

Drip Irrigation

Drip irrigation is as effective and convenient for quenching the thirst of trees, shrubs, and vines as it is for quenching the thirst of any other cultivated plants. One difference when using the drip method with woody plants is that you must change the watering schedule over the years, as the plants grow. Right after planting, for example, a potted tree needs its original root ball thoroughly soaked every day, just as it probably was in the nursery. Intervals between waterings are then gradually extended as roots spread into the surrounding soil.

Also, a single drip emitter might provide sufficient water to meet the needs of only a small plant. As the plant grows, more emitters or a loop of dripper-line, (in-line emitter tubing) are needed to both spread out the applied water and drip more of it. Emitters also will have to be placed farther from the plant as feeder roots grow outward.

If a tree, shrub, or vine is well matched to its site and climate, irrigation (drip or otherwise) will eventually not be needed at all. In this case, diligent hand-watering for a year or two might be preferable to going through the trouble of temporarily installing drip irrigation.

applied over undisturbed mowed ground.

Trees 10 or more feet high and bushes with many stems, especially in windy sites, need to be staked for a year until their roots grab firm hold of the soil. One stake set in the ground on the side of prevailing winds suffices for small plants (trees with trunks less than 2 inches in diameter), but two stakes on either side of the plant are better for medium-size plants. Use three guy wires anchored to the ground for large trees. Any tying material *must* be soft or padded. But don't coddle trees too much with staking, attempting to quell all movement or keep stakes in place for years. Movement helps thicken and strengthen a trunk, so anchor it low enough to allow some movement.

Remove the support once the plant seems rigid enough at the soil line, usually after a year.

The thin bark of many young trees, especially those native to woodlands, is apt to get damaged when moved to a sunny backyard. Sunscald results from a sudden drop in bark temperature as the sun sets on cold, clear winter days or from intense summer sun in hot climates. In cold climates, prevent sunscald by wrapping the trunk with paper tree wrap, plastic coils, tape sold for this purpose, or by brushing on white latex paint. Remove any wrappings in spring or they will create safe and cozy homes for bark-loving insects. In hot climates, bark protection for young trees is obviously needed in summer.

The final step to complete your planting is watering. Slowly and thoroughly soaking the ground beneath your new plant gives it a drink and further settles the soil. Provide about one gallon per week per square-foot spread of the roots while the plant is establishing itself.

Once the plant is in the ground and watered, don't turn your back on it. Reestablishment of a tree, shrub, or vine takes time, especially for larger plants and where cool climates slow root growth. About a year is needed for each inch of trunk thickness to reestablish a tree in northern climates; only three months per inch of trunk diameter is needed in subtropical climates. Because small plants establish themselves more quickly, in time they can catch up

A happy young tree with a shallow, broad planting hole, a slight mound for drainage, and a temporary stake.

with or even surpass growth of plants that are initially larger. (So take your pick: Do you want a larger plant sooner or later?) After the first year, spread fertilizer on top of the ground, if needed (up to the equivalent of $6/10$ pound of actual nitrogen for each 100-square-foot spread of the branches).

Water is usually the single most important factor limiting the growth of a young tree, shrub, or vine. As stems grow, they transpire increasing amounts of water that become more than offset by what growing roots garner as they explore more soil. With time, gradually increase the intervals between waterings, but never to less than the equivalent of one gallon per week per square-foot spread of the roots. Water diligently the entire first season, aware that the soil surrounding an initially balled-and-burlapped or potted plant might be moist even if the original root mass, where most of the roots still are, is dry. After all, when growing in a pot at a nursery, that plant might have been watered almost every day.

For at least a few years, keep the mulched circle around your tree weed-free and add mulch as needed. You may even want to keep the ground permanently mulched or planted with some ground cover. Besides keeping weeds at bay and conserving moisture, an area that is mulched also keeps lawnmowers and weed whackers at bay, both of which are hazardous to young plants.

Maintenance

It's hard to say when the establishment phase for a tree, shrub, or vine ends and the maintenance phase begins. It depends on the initial size of the plant, the growing conditions, and the length of the growing season. Plan on a few years before a woody plant can fully

Mousy Threats

The soft, moist mulched ground that woody plants love so much also makes a fine home for mice; and mice feeding on plant roots and bark can spell death to young plants, and weaken or even kill old plants. Luckily, there are ways to thwart these creatures.

Even if soft mulch provides such a nice shelter for mice, the rest of the environment doesn't have to. Mow any lawn growing beyond the mulched area at a low height, and mice will think twice before scooting across the grass in view of hawks and other predators. Some gardeners report that a 2-foot-diameter circle of pea-gravel right around the trunk of a tree keeps burrowing mice at bay, or that these vegetarian rodents won't munch on bark coated in winter with a mix of white latex paint and bonemeal (the white paint prevents sunscald).

Mice cannot get to trunks protected by hardware cloth.

The most reliable rodent protection right at the tree is a cylinder of quarter-inch or half-inch wire mesh, 2 feet high, sunk a couple of inches into the ground. I make my cylinders 18 inches in diameter to allow plenty of room for growth and so that I can easily reach down inside to pull weeds. Bark wrappings of aluminum foil, paper, or plastic spirals made for this purpose are also effective, but less so.

Two other possibilities, both less popular with the mice, are cats and poison baits, the latter placed in tubes inaccessible to other animals and, of course, kept away from children.

fend for itself, and even after that, check on it occasionally.

How you take care of the ground (and this includes dealing with weeds) beneath an established tree, vine, or shrub is going to represent a melding of your aesthetic vision with what is practical and what is good for the plant and soil. The underpinning for your apple trees is not necessarily going to be the same as for your maple tree or wisteria vine.

From the point of view of any woody plant, the ideal is to have ground blanketed with some organic material at least as wide as the above-ground spread of the branches—or even wider, because roots commonly spread beyond the shadow of the branches.

The Lawn Option

Lawn grass might be what you want beneath that stately maple gracing your front lawn. It is certainly nicer to sit on than wood chips, and you'd have a hard time knocking a croquet ball around ground strewn with straw.

Lawn grass is a viable option for Weedless Gardening with any tree, vine, or shrub—with some reservations. First, choose a plant appropriate for growing in lawn grass. Don't expect grass to endure beneath a beech tree, for instance. The large, shallow roots of beech trees eventually ooze above the surface of the ground, making mowing difficult for you and damaging to the tree. Wide-spreading low branches compound the difficulty of mowing. Lawn will eventually disappear beneath any tree or large shrub that casts deep shade, a characteristic for which Norway maples, for example, are notorious.

Lawn grasses are fierce competitors for nutrients and water. As a result, trees, shrubs, and vines growing in lawn need more water and nutrients than those growing in mulched ground. So keep an eye on

Soil Injection

It's another one of those nifty gadgets that seem so logically effective: a root feeder that injects fertilizer into the soil, getting the fertilizer down to tree and shrub roots without feeding the lawn in which these plants are growing. Or so the logic goes.

True, those tree and shrub roots are competing with the grass for nutrients and water. But the roots of all these plants are in just about the same depth of soil, so injecting fertilizer deep into the soil is not an effective way to selectively feed trees and shrubs. Better to weaken the grass with more aggressive mowing and/or to add more fertilizer if it's needed.

the plant, and apply food or water as needed right on top of the grass—you're still caring for the soil from the top down.

A mower or weed whacker can present a threat even to the bark of established trees, shrubs, and vines, especially to those whose bark is naturally thin. This makes a good case for keeping that mulched circle at the base of a plant even after it is well established—a narrow ring keeps the cutting implements at bay.

Other Plants

An attractive alternative to an underplanting of lawn grass is a mixed underplanting, whereby a tree, shrub, and/or vine could mingle with woody plants in addition to flowers. In this case, treat the ground as you would for a mixed flower border.

Another option for underplanting a tree, shrub, or vine is a sweep of decorative ground cover. Here, maintenance requirements are reduced mostly to pulling occasional weeds—much the same as it would be for a ground cover alone. Decorative ground covers are not nearly as hungry for water and nutrients as grasses are, so the tree, shrub, or vine hardly knows they're underfoot; nonetheless, keep an eye on the plant for symptoms of hunger or thirst, especially when it's young.

A third possibility for underplanting is one or more cover-crop plants. Some cover crops—crimson clover, for example—are decorative as well as utilitarian (see pages 50–51 for a list of cover crops). Of course, many cover crops are strictly utilitarian, which limits their use to fruiting trees, shrubs, and vines. Because these plants offer a harvest and need to have their vegetative and fruiting growth balanced, they generally put greater demands on the soil than strictly ornamental plants.

The frequency and height of mowing of a surrounding cover crop can regulate the growth of a tree, shrub, or vine planted therein, just as it can with lawn grass—even more so, depending on what plant(s) are chosen for their particular strengths. For example, legumes garner atmospheric nitrogen, rye grain sucks up extra nitrogen, sweet clovers loosen subsoil, and buckwheat chokes out weeds.

Any plants chosen to grow beneath a tree, shrub, or vine also might influence pests, from large mammals down to almost microscopic mites. Crown vetch was once recommended as a ground cover for apple orchards, but had to be abandoned because it provided appetizers or desserts for deer—before or after they browsed on the apple trees. In West Coast orchards, legumes can increase nematode problems and overgrown cover crops can encourage stink bugs and lygus bugs.

On the other hand, besides their indirect benefits to plant health via the soil, many cover crops provide habitat and alternate food sources for beneficial insects and mites (to tide these good guys over until they find and start chomping on the bad guys). Buckwheat, crimson clover, red clover, and many vetches are among the star cover crops for attracting beneficial insects. Grape growers in California plant mixtures of barley and vetch for this purpose and to help rebuff

How French!

If you've ever strolled through Les Jardins des Tuileries in Paris, you saw yet another method of ground management beneath large trees. There, the surface of the ground is nothing more than fine white gravel. No ground cover, no lawn, no shrubs, no weeds. The surface is evidently kept as is by a combination of constant foot traffic, shade, lack of weed seeds because of the large expanse of weed-free area, no digging, and perhaps occasional raking—not conditions you would find in the average backyard.

leafhoppers. To round out pest-preventing benefits of ground-cover plants, throw into the mix some other plants whose floral nectar feeds beneficial insects, such as members of the daisy family (marigolds, asters, fleabanes, and others, including any of a number of "daisies") and the carrot family (carrot, parsley, angelica, celery, and fennel). Management, plant choice, and observation are the keys to getting the most from cover crops grown beneath woody plants, and there are many exciting possibilities for experimentation.

Mulch Thanks

From the point of view of the plant and the soil, a permanent organic mulch spread wide over the ground is ideal. All my trees and shrubs get this treatment when young, but only my prize fruit trees get coddled with this treatment forever. After all, they have the heaviest demands put upon them—having to pump out large, luscious fruits year after year.

A large mulched area beneath trees need not be an eyesore. My planting of 22 dwarf apple trees, each a different variety, lined up and curving gracefully to a grove of bamboo at the rear of my backyard, looks neat and trim with the ground beneath blanketed in one continuous swath of wood chips. To be honest, I have planted something else in those wood chips: two varieties of species tulips, which liven the tawny floor first with scarlet and then with yellow blossoms each spring.

Maintenance of mulched ground beneath any tree, shrub, or vine is minimal. Each year, preferably in autumn or early spring, I spread a few of inches of new chips over the old ones beneath my apple trees. A naturally rich soil and almost two decades of toppings of wood chips—and sometimes autumn leaves—now provide all the nutrients the plants need. In poor soil, either fertilizer spread on top of the mulch or a mulch of compost would provide needed nutrition. The mulched soil beneath my apple trees stays sufficiently moist so that for over a decade, I have not turned on the drip irrigation.

Apple trees are here mulched in a continuous bed of wood chips, with some tulips for spring color.

Perhaps twice during the growing season, to keep creeping Charlie and quackgrass from interloping, I will tidy up the edge where the chips meet the lawn. Within the mulched area, time spent weeding amounts to perhaps five or ten minutes— for the whole season!

EPILOGUE

The last word has not been said (or written) about weeds. Gardening and farming create weeds by altering the plans of Mother Nature; she is far more persistent than any of us.

The more closely we follow Nature's lead, though, the less we fight her. In Weedless Gardening, we emulate natural conditions in the garden by minimizing soil disruption and compaction, and by keeping the surface of the ground protected. If we then pinpoint watering according to location and need, weeds cease to be garden spectres. Weeding becomes just another pleasant garden activity.

Yes, occasional problems will arise with Weedless Gardening. In my garden, moles thrived in the undisturbed, rich earth, their tunnels disrupting plants. Cat and/or mole repellents such as castor oil or mole plant *(Euphorbia lathyrus)* took care of this problem. Bean beetles were also a problem, perhaps because they enjoyed nooks and crannies of undisturbed soil and the season-long forage offered by pole beans. Successive crops of bush beans, with a thorough cleanup just before each larvae hatch, now keeps this pest in check.

The basics of Weedless Gardening have been spelled out. For the future let's fine-tune details such as making better use of cover crops and integrating ornamental and edible plantings. The last word has not been said (or written) about Weedless Gardening either.

Gardens change over time, through the season and through the years, as does the character of the soil and the weeds therein. Give Weedless Gardening a try for at least a couple of years—you'll be amazed at the health of your plants and how weed problems recede into a dim memory.

APPENDIX ONE

Soil Testing

Existing plant growth can tell you something about the fertility and acidity of a soil. Rampant weeds or lush lawns generally indicate that all is well. Specific plants can lend support to such observations and divulge more.

Some weeds/wild plants that colonize nutrient-rich soils include stinging nettle, wild garlic, quackgrass, pigweed, common burdock, English daisy, yellow rocket, common teasel, curly dock, and bedstraw. Clovers, lupines, yarrow, spotted knapweed, yellow hawkweed, bird's-foot trefoil, and black medic are usually indicative of hungry soils. You'll often find cinquefoil, coltsfoot, hawkweed, horsetail, mullein, stinging nettle, plantain, sorrel, blueberry, mountain laurel, hemlock, and/or wild strawberry growing in acidic soils. Bellflower, campion, Queen Anne's lace, black henbane, and pennycress are common denizens of alkaline soils.

The quantitative way to determine what is in your soil and its acidity (pH) is with a soil test. Most important to getting an accurate soil test is the sampling procedure itself (see Appendix Two, page 188, for details on sampling). An initial soil test, while not absolutely necessary, helps assure that your plants get off to a good start. If you follow the methods described in this book, subsequent testing will be unnecessary—except for the pleasure of confirming how healthy your soil is.

Testing can be done by you or by a private or state testing laboratory, and there are numerous testing options. At the very least, test soil

Soil Testing Laboratories

- State Laboratories (contacted through your local Cooperative Extension Service)

- A & L Eastern Agricultural Laboratories
7621 White Pine Road
Richmond, VA 23237
804-743-9401

- Peaceful Valley Farm Supply
P.O. Box 2209
Grass Valley, CA 95945
888-784-1722
www.groworganic.com

- Wallace Laboratories
365 Coral Circle
El Segundo, CA 90254
310-615-0116
www.wallacelabs.com

acidity. You also might want to test for phosphorus and potassium, both of which plants require in relatively large amounts. Other so-called macronutrients that you might test for include calcium, magnesium, and sulfur. A complete checkup also includes testing for micronutrients, such as iron, manganese, and zinc, which are essential but required in only minute quantities.

Soil tests rarely determine nitrogen, even though this is the nutrient for which plants are most hungry. Most soil nitrogen is locked up in organic matter and the amount available to plants waxes and wanes as weather conditions influence decomposition. Nitrogen is also readily lost from soil, puffed away as a gas or leached by rainfall beyond the reach of roots. The stuff is simply too evanescent to make testing for it meaningful at any one point in time.

When your soil test is complete, you will receive information about your soil's organic matter, texture (clay, silt, sand, etc.), acidity, and levels of specific nutrients. You will also get a recommendation for fertilizer, and for lime or sulfur to raise or lower the pH. Fertilizer recommendations are based on what is in the soil and what kinds of plants you intend to grow. In the case of nitrogen, recommendations generally reflect particular crops' needs rather than a soil test.

Test reports usually give recommendations for some common fertilizer, such as 10-10-10 or 5-10-5, the sets of three numbers representing percentages of nitrogen, phosphorus, and potassium. Follow fertilizer recommendations closely for amounts of nutrients because too much can be as harmful as too little, causing nutrient imbalances, even death, to plants. Feel free to choose any type of fertilizer (differing in concentration from that recommended, and organic rather than synthetic) that supplies the recommended amounts of nitrogen, phosphorus, and potassium.

> ## Sources for Home Soil-Test Kits
>
> • Gardener's Supply Co.
> 128 Intervale Road
> Burlington, VT 05401
> 800-833-1412
> www.gardeners.com
>
> • Gemplers
> 100 Countryside Drive
> P.O. Box 270
> Belleville, WI 53508
> 800-382-8473
> www.gemplers.com
>
> • Mellingers
> 2310 West South Range Road
> North Lima, OH 44452
> 800-321-7444
> www.mellingers.com

APPENDIX TWO

Taking a Soil Sample

ow you collect the sample itself is crucial to the accuracy of any soil test. In even a modest-size garden of a 100 square feet, one cup of soil—the amount used for the test—

represents only 0.001 percent of the top 6 inches of soil. Therefore, the sample must be truly representative of the whole area to be tested.

The test area should be relatively uniform. Areas devoted to very different kinds of plants—vegetables and lawn, for example—require separate samples. (Vegetable and flower gardens can be sampled together, though.) If your garden or lawn is big enough to include obvious differences in soil or topography, subdivide the area into separate areas, and test each one separately.

Avoid nonrepresentative samples even within your uniform test area. Do not sample near garden fences, walls, or other borders. Or where your compost pile was two years ago. Or where you filled your fertilizer spreader with lime. To even out small differences over even relatively uniform soil, take a half-dozen samples from random spots.

Generally, sample to a depth of 6 inches. Remove any surface debris, such as wood chips, compost, and plant residues, or the sod itself in the case of an established lawn, before making a hole to the required depth.

Don't use that first trowelful of soil. It's cone-shaped, with a greater proportion of soil from the surface than from lower down. Take a slice, uniformly thick from top to bottom, from along the edge of that hole you just made. Alternately, use a soil sampling tube to get samples of full width for the whole depth.

As you gather samples from each test area, put them together into a clean plastic bucket. Thoroughly mix the composited soil to average out differences among samples, crumbling it and discarding stones, sticks, insects, and other debris as you mix. Spread the soil out on a clean baking pan to air-dry for a day, then remove about a cup for testing. Throughout your sample preparation, avoid contamination from dirty hands or utensils.

Carefully follow any instructions supplied by the laboratory about packing the soil if you are sending the sample out for testing. If you are testing more than one area, label samples from each area and record for yourself the locations on your property. Equally important is to supply the laboratory with any information requested about fertilization history, as well as what you intend to grow. Indicate whether you wish any special tests, such as for micronutrients or toxic elements (such as lead) in the soil.

APPENDIX THREE
Further Reading

INTRODUCTION: HOW WE GOT HERE

Faulkner, Edward. *Plowman's Folly.* Norman, Okla.: University of Oklahoma Press, 1943.

Fukuoka, Masanobu. *The One-Straw Revolution.* Emmaus, Pa.: Rodale Press, 1978.

Kourik, Robert. *Designing and Maintaining Your Edible Landscape Naturally.* Santa Rosa, Cal.: Metamorphic Press, 1986.

Lanza, Patricia. *Lasagna Gardening.* Emmaus, Pa.: Rodale Press, 1998.

Little, Charles. *Green Fields Forever: The Conservation Tillage Revolution in America.* Washington, D.C.: Island Press, 1987.

Nye, P. H., and D. J. Greenland. "The Soil Under Shifting Cultivation." *Technical Communication,* No. 51, Commonwealth Agricultural Bureaux, Bucks, England, 1960.

O'Brien, R. Dalziel. *Intensive Gardening.* New York: Faber and Faber, 1956.

Poincelot Raymond. *Toward a More Sustainable Agriculture.* AVI Publishing, 1986.

Stout, Ruth, and Richard Clemence. *The Ruth Stout No-Work Garden Book.* Emmaus, Pa.: Rodale Press, 1971.

CHAPTER ONE: WHY GARDEN FROM THE TOP DOWN?

Atkinson, D., et al. *Tree Root Systems and Their Mycorrhizas.* The Hague: Martinus Nijhoff/Dr. W. Junk Publishers, 1983.

Buhler, Douglas. "Effect of Tillage and Light Environment on Emergence of 13 Annual Weeds."

Weed Technology, 11:496–501, 1997.

Magdoff, Fred, and Harold van Es. *Building Soils for Better Crops,* 2nd ed. Burlington, Vt.: Sustainable Agriculture Network, 2000.

Sullivan, Preston. *Principles of Sustainable Weed Management.* Appropriate Technology Transfer for Rural Areas (ATTRA), 1999.

CHAPTER TWO: IN THE BEGINNING: READYING THE GROUND FOR A FIRST-TIME PLANTING

Foth, H. D., and L. M. Turk. *Fundamentals of Soil Science,* 5th ed. New York: John Wiley & Sons, 1972.

Glenn, D. M., and W. V. Welker. "Cultural Practices for Enhanced Growth of Young Peach Trees." *American Journal of Alternative Agriculture* 4(1):8–11, 1989.

Hill, Stuart, and Jennifer Ramsay. "Weeds as Indicators of Soil Conditions." *The MacDonald Journal,* June 1977.

Kourik, Robert. *Designing and Maintaining Your Edible Landscape Naturally.* Santa Clara, Cal.: Metamorphic Press, 1986.

Pfeiffer, E. *Weeds and What They Tell.* Biodynamic Farming & Gardening Association, 1981.

CHAPTER THREE: THROUGH THE YEAR IN THE WEEDLESS GARDEN

Magdoff, Fred, and Harold van Es. *Building Soils for Better Crops,* 2nd ed. Burlington, Vt.: Sustainable Agriculture Network, 2000.

Managing Cover Crops Profitably, 2nd ed. Burlington, Vt.: Sustainable Agriculture Network, 1998.

Sarrantonio, Marianne. *Northeast Cover Crop Handbook.* Kutztown, Pa.: Rodale Institute, 1994.

CHAPTER FOUR: COAXING PLANTS FURTHER ALONG

Golueke, Clarence. *Composting, A Study of the Process and Its Principles.* Emmaus, Pa.: Rodale Press, 1972.

Kourik, Robert. *Drip Irrigation for Every Landscape and All Climates.* Santa Rosa, Cal.: Metamorphic Press, 1992.

Magdoff, Fred, and Harold van Es. *Building Soils for Better Crops,* 2nd ed. Burlington, Vt.: Sustainable Agriculture Network, 2000.

Ross, D. S., R. A. Parsons, and H. E. Carpenter. "Trickle Irrigation in the Eastern United States." NRAES 4. Ithaca, N.Y.: *Northeast Regional Agricultural Engineering Service,* 1985.

The Complete Book of Composting. Staff of *Organic Gardening and Farming* magazine. Emmaus, Pa.: Rodale Press, 1967.

Urban Home Composting. Vancouver, B.C.: City Farmer, Canada's Office of Urban Agriculture, 1993.

CHAPTER FIVE: A CORNUCOPIA OF DELECTABLE VEGETABLES

Coleman, Eliot. *Four-Season Harvest: How to Harvest Fresh Organic Vegetables from Your Home Garden All Year Long.* White River Junction, Vt.: Chelsea Green Publishing Co., 1992.

———*The New Organic Grower: A Master's Manual of Tools and Techniques for the Home and Market Gardener,* 2nd ed. White River Junction, Vt.: Chelsea Green Publishing Co., 1995.

Fox, Helen M. *Gardening for Good Eating.* New York: Collier Books, 1973.

National Gardening Association. *Gardening: The Complete Guide to Growing America's Favorite Fruits & Vegetables.* Addison-Wesley Publishing, 1986.

Rodale, Robert, ed. *The Basic Book of Organic Gardening.* New York: Ballantine Books, 1971.

Watts, R. L., and G. S. Watts. *The Vegetable Growing Business.* New York: Orange Judd Publishing, 1954.

CHAPTER SIX: FLOWER GARDENS AND HERBACEOUS GROUND COVERS

Martin, Laura. *The Wildflower Meadow Book.* Charlotte, N.C.: East Woods Press, 1986.

Pauly, Wayne. *How to Manage Small Prairie Fires.* Madison, Wis.: Dane County Park Commission, 1988.

Springer, Lauren. *The Undaunted Garden.* Golden, Colo.: Fulcrum Publishing, 1994.

Still, Steven. *Manual of Herbaceous Ornamental Plants.* Champagne, Ill.: Stipes Publishing Co., 1994.

CHAPTER SEVEN: TREES, SHRUBS, AND VINES, INCLUDING FRUIT PLANTS

Dirr, Michael. *Manual of Woody Landscape Plants.* Champagne, Ill.: Stipes Publishing, 1990.

Kourik, Robert. *Designing and Maintaining Your Edible Landscape Naturally.* Santa Rosa, Cal.: Metamorphic Press, 1986.

Pirrone, P. P. *Tree Maintenance.* New York: Oxford University Press, 1978.

Reich, Lee. *Growing Fruit in Your Backyard.* New York: Macmillan Publishing, 1996.

Watson, Gary, and E. B. Himelick. *Principles and Practices of Planting Trees and Shrubs.* International Society of Arboriculture, 1997.

INDEX